OCCASIONAL PAPER 141

Monetary and Exchange System Reforms in China
An Experiment in Gradualism

Hassanali Mehran, Marc Quintyn,
Tom Nordman, and Bernard Laurens

INTERNATIONAL MONETARY FUND
Washington DC
September 1996

Library of Congress Cataloging-in-Publication Data

Monetary and exchange system reforms in China : an experiment in gradualism / Hassanali Mehran . . . [et al.]. —
    p. cm. — (Occasional Paper ; 141)
    Includes bibliographical references.
    ISBN 1-55775-562-0
    1. Finance — China. 2. Monetary policy — China. 3. Banks and
banking — China. 4. China — Economic policy — 1976– I. Mehran,
Hassanali. II.Series: Occasional paper (International Monetary Fund) ;
no.141.
HG187.C3M66   1996
332.1'0951—dc20   96-34203
                                              CIP

Price: US$15.00
(US$12.00 to full-time faculty members and
students at universities and colleges)

Please send orders to:
International Monetary Fund, Publication Services
700 19th Street, N.W., Washington, D.C. 20431, U.S.A.
Tel.: (202) 623-7430   Telefax: (202) 623-7201
Internet: publications@imf.org

recycled paper

Contents

Boxes
Section

Tables
Section

Charts Section

The following symbols have been used throughout this paper:

. . .   to indicate that data are not available;

—   to indicate that the figure is zero or less than half the final digit shown, or that the item does not exist;

–   between years or months (e.g., 1991–92 or January–June) to indicate the years or months covered, including the beginning and ending years or months;

/   between years (e.g., 1991/92) to indicate a crop or fiscal (financial) year.

"Billion" means a thousand million.

Minor discrepancies between constituent figures and totals are due to rounding.

The term "country," as used in this paper, does not in all cases refer to a territorial entity that is a state as understood by international law and practice; the term also covers some territorial entities that are not states, but for which statistical data are maintained and provided internationally on a separate and independent basis.

Preface

This IMF Occasional Paper traces the monetary, exchange, and financial sector developments in China since 1978, when the country embarked upon a far-reaching reform of its economic system. The paper reflects the continuous involvement of its authors, as well as of a number of other IMF staff and outside consultants on China, going back to 1991. The staff advisory work in the areas covered by this paper initially focused on central banking and commercial banking legislation, with contributions by Tobias Asser (Assistant General Counsel, Legal Department), and with the participation of Manuel Guitián and Justin Zulu (Directors, Monetary and Exchange Affairs Department (MAE)), William Holder (Deputy General Counsel), Leonard Gleske (member of the Board, Bundesbank), Didier Bruneel (Secretary General, Bank of France), Akira Nambara (Executive Director, Bank of Japan), and J. De Beaufort Wijnholds (Executive Director, IMF), as well as Hassanali Mehran and Marc Quintyn. Bernard Laurens integrated the material into the section dealing with legal issues in this paper.

The development of the exchange markets reflects a series of missions and parallel workshops organized for this purpose. Masaru Tanaka, Yoshihiko Noguchi, and Shuzo Sakata (Bank of Japan), David Strachan (Bank of England), Christopher Mc-Curdy and Dino Kos (Federal Reserve Bank of New York), Thanasak Chantarovas (Bank of Thailand), and Igor Kniazev (Central Bank of the Russian Federation) participated at various times and contributed to the process. Tom Nordman, who headed these missions, put together the section on the development of the exchange system. R. Barry Johnston, Arto Kovanen, and Bernard Laurens also participated and contributed at various stages.

The sections on financial sector, money and capital market development, and instruments of monetary policy are the product of a series of missions, seminars, and workshops that were organized in China and in which, in addition to Hassanali Mehran, Marc Quintyn, and Bernard Laurens, a number of experts from the cooperating central banks participated. They were Ian Clunie (Bank of Canada), Leonard Fernelius (formerly Federal Reserve Bank of Minneapolis), Giorgio Gobbi (Bank of Italy), Jae-Chun Kim (Bank of Korea), Suchada Kirakul (Bank of Thailand), Werner Nimmerrichter (Bundesbank), Irwin Sandberg (formerly Federal Reserve Bank of New York), Rüsdü Saraçoglu (formerly Governor, Central Bank of the Republic of Turkey), Hiroki Tanaka (Bank of Japan), and Abdul Ghani Zamani (Bank Negara Malaysia). Professor Maxwell Fry also conducted seminars on money demand estimates and reserve money programming. Payments, clearing, and settlement systems were the subject of one workshop in which Leonard Fernelius participated. The theme of one mission in which Eung-Jin Kim (Bank of Korea) participated was currency issue and management. Marc Quintyn integrated these sections, as well as the paper as a whole. The statistical work has been coordinated by Bernard Laurens, while tables and charts have been prepared by Kiran Sastry (Research Assistant, MAE). Charmion O'Connor (Administrative Assistant, MAE) prepared the manuscript, and Thomas Walter (External Relations Department) skillfully edited the text and coordinated its production and publication.

Throughout the work of various missions and in the final stage of preparing this paper, Douglas Scott, the IMF Resident Representative in China, worked closely with the staff and contributed greatly to the policy discussions with the authorities. He also extensively commented on all sections of the paper.

The staff of the People's Bank of China and of the State Administration for Exchange Control cooperated closely with the IMF teams during their work in China. The Chinese officials maintained frank and open discussions, presenting to the IMF staff the policy options for China in the area of financial sector reform. To them, who are too numerous to name here, the special thanks of the authors are due. Our special thanks are also due to Governor Dai Xianglong and Deputy Governor Chen Yuan, who coordinated the work of the missions' counterpart teams.

The authors are also grateful to their colleagues in several IMF departments who provided useful comments and suggestions on earlier drafts of this paper. They are particularly grateful to their MAE colleagues Ales Bulir, Peter Dattels, Anne-Marie Gulde, Kyung Mo Huh, V. Sundararajan, and Peter J. Winglee for their helpful suggestions and insights.

The views expressed in this Occasional Paper, as well as any remaining errors, are the sole responsibility of the authors and do not necessarily reflect the opinions of the Chinese Government, the Executive Directors of the IMF, or any other members of the IMF staff.

Glossary of Abbreviations

ABC	Agricultural Bank of China
BOC	Bank of China
BOCOM	Bank of Communications
CFETS	China Foreign Exchange Trade System
CIB	China Investment Bank
CITIC	China International Trust and Investment Corporation
EIS	Electronic Interbank System
FEACs	Foreign Exchange Adjustment Centers (swap centers)
FFEs	foreign-funded enterprises
ICBC	Industrial and Commercial Bank of China
ITICs	international trust and investment companies
MOFERT	Ministry of Foreign Economic Relations and Trade
NBFIs	nonbank financial institutions
NETS	National Electronic Trading System
NFEAC	National Foreign Exchange Adjustment Center
OTC	over-the-counter
PBC	People's Bank of China
PCBC	People's Construction Bank of China
PSSS	Provisional Securities Settlement System
PICC	People's Insurance Company of China
RCCs	rural credit cooperatives
RMB	renminbi
SAEC	State Administration for Exchange Control
SEZs	Special Economic Zones
SOEs	state-owned enterprises
STAQS	Securities Trading Automated Quotations System
TICs	trust and investment companies
TVEs	township and village enterprises
UCCs	urban credit cooperatives

I Introduction

In 1978, China embarked on a gradual but far-reaching reform of its economic system. In December 1978, the Third Plenum of the Eleventh Central Committee of the Communist Party identified the principal contradiction in China's social, political, and economic system as the backwardness of the economy in responding to the needs of the people. Therefore, the principal task was to reform those aspects of the economic system that had impeded the development of the economy.[1]

In the decade and a half that has elapsed since the start of the reform process, China's economy has been significantly modernized and opened to the rest of the world. In addition, the concept of reform itself has evolved. The most dramatic change in it took place in 1992, when the Communist Party formally embraced the view that the market system was not incompatible with the ideals of socialism and proclaimed the idea of establishing a "socialist market economy." The concept of a socialist market economy implies an economy in which the market mechanism governs economic interactions but ownership over the most important means of production remains in the hands of the public sector or the collectivity, thus preserving the socialist character of the society.

In October 1992, the Fourteenth Party Congress adopted this idea as China's official line for the future. In the wake of this decision, the Third Plenum of the Fourteenth Central Committee (November 1993) outlined and approved a comprehensive reform strategy aimed at achieving a breakthrough in China's efforts to transform its economy into a market-based system.[2] More than in preceding reforms, this reform program derives much of its significance from its definition of clear objectives and adoption of a comprehensive and consistent package of reform measures to realize the framework of the socialist market economy by the year 2000.

The contrast with previous reform goals is perhaps clearest in the financial sector. The November 1993 program explicitly mentioned financial reform as a key element to ensure the creation of efficient financial markets in order to strengthen the capability for macroeconomic management through indirect instruments. Box 1 provides a summary overview of the decision of the Third Plenum regarding the financial sector. Implicitly, this statement recognized that the financial sector, if not reformed, could become a bottleneck for further reforms in other parts of the Chinese economy.

This paper takes a closer look at the process of reforming China's monetary and foreign exchange system, describing the achievements so far and analyzing the task ahead to achieve the goals set for 2000. Section II provides an overview of the main achievements thus far and places financial reform within the general reform framework. Sections III through VIII give a detailed account of the reform process in, respectively, the financial sector, the legal framework for financial transactions, financial markets, the payments system, and the monetary policy and foreign exchange system. Section IX discusses the outlook for further reform, and the main conclusions of this paper are presented in Section X.

---

[1]See, among others, Bell, Khor, and Kochhar (1993) and Perkins (1988).

[2]Decision of the Third Plenum of the Fourteenth Central Committee on Issues Concerning the Establishment of Socialist Market Structure.

Box 1. Decision of the Third Plenum On Financial Development

Guided by the theory of building "socialism with Chinese characteristics," great changes occurred in China's economic structure in the period 1978–92, as the role of the market in the distribution of resources rapidly expanded. The decision of the Third Plenary Session of the 14th Central Committee of the Communist Party of China of November 14, 1993, however, meant a break with past reforms, as for the first time a blueprint was presented to guide future reforms. The decision of the Plenary Session explicitly laid down the goals of establishing a socialist market economy by the end of the century, thereby allowing the market to play the decisive role in resource allocation under macroeconomic control by the state. The decision of the Third Plenum is thus a milestone in China's economic reform process.

To achieve the goal of establishing a structure conducive to the operation of a socialist market economy and to accelerate the pace of transformation, a number of areas in which further reforms were deemed necessary were specifically indicated, including reform of the state-owned enterprises; transformation of government functions; establishment of a sound macroeconomic control system and of a rural system of income distribution and social security; deepening of the rural economic structural reforms; further revamping of the educational system; and tightening of the legal framework.

The contrast with previous reforms is perhaps clearest in the financial sector. The decision explicitly mentions that "the present cultivation of the market system should focus on the development of markets for finance . . . ." Both capital and money markets are mentioned: "Capital markets should actively but steadily expand financing activities in the form of bonds and stocks"; and "the money market should develop standard interbank lending and bill discount." This was an implicit recognition that the financial sector, if not reformed, could become a bottleneck for further reforms in other parts of the Chinese economy.

The decision of the Third Plenum explicitly mentions that the establishment of a "sound macroeconomic control system" requires the establishment of a "central bank whose primary objective is to stabilize currency value, regulate the aggregate money supply, and maintain balance of international payments." Accelerating reform of the financial system requires that "the central bank, the People's Bank of China, under the leadership of the State Council, should implement monetary policies independently." Moreover, "the power of the central bank and local authorities over economic administration should be rationally delineated," and "powers of macroeconomic control, which

include power over the issuance of currency, the determination of benchmark interest rates, regulation of the exchange rate . . . , must be concentrated in the hands of the central government." One practical consequence is that "the branches of the People's Bank of China are certified as agencies of its head office."

On the conduct of monetary policy, the decision provides detailed guidelines. The central bank "should control the money supply and stabilize currency value by changing from relying mainly on the control over the scale of credit to using such means as reserve ratio on deposits, the central bank's lending rates, and open market operations." Moreover, "in light of the changes in the monetary supply and demand, the central bank should make timely readjustments of the benchmark interest rate and allow the deposit and loan interest rates of commercial banks to float freely within a specified range." These provisions underline the determination of the authorities to shift resolutely from direct to indirect monetary management. On the foreign exchange system, the goal is "to set up a market-based, managed floating system, and an integrated and standardized foreign exchange market," with the renminbi (the currency of China) "becoming gradually a convertible currency."

With respect to the coordination of monetary and fiscal policies, the decision mentions that "the fiscal deficit of the central authorities should be met by issuing long- and short-term government bonds rather than by overdrafts from the central bank." Also, "the government's domestic and external debts should be centrally managed." These provisions, which pave the way for active domestic debt management through the issuance of government securities, are consistent with the decision to develop open market operations.

Regarding the banking sector, policy lending banks should be established in order "to separate policy lending banking from commercial banking." The decision mentions the establishment of the National Development Bank and of the Import and Export Credit Bank, as well as the reorganization of the Agricultural Bank of China, to handle strictly policy-related business. New commercial banks should be established and "the existing specialized banks should gradually transform into commercial banks." Moreover, "the commercial banks should engage in the management of the proportions of assets and liabilities and in the management of risks." These provisions aim at enhancing the commercialization of the banking system. The provisions that nonbank financial institutions (NBFIs) should be standardized and developed underline the desire to better monitor the activities of the NBFIs. Finally, "banking business and securities business should be managed along separate lines."

II China's Financial Reforms Since 1978: An Overview

Given the country's history and size, China's reform process thus far has been a unique experience. The transformation of China's economy started at a much earlier date than the reform of similar economic systems of Eastern Europe and the Baltic states, Russia, and other countries of the former Soviet Union. China's reforms have been gradual, and the starting position was very different from that of other command economies that decided to transform their systems.[3] In some respects, as described in Box 2, China's economic transformation resembles more the modernization of some East Asian economies than that of many former centrally planned economies. Table 1 presents a detailed comparison of financial sector policies and development in China, Northeast Asia, and Southeast Asia.

The resemblance to some Southeast Asian success stories is most noticeable in the underlying conditions of the reform process, that is, the macroeconomic stability and high savings ratio. Similarly, China adopted a pragmatic and gradual strategy toward reform. In several Southeast Asian countries, controls over market mechanisms were typically removed only slowly and sometimes reintroduced when the economy tended to overheat. Another striking similarity between the modernization process in China and in some neighboring countries is that the modernization—or "marketization"—of the financial system was slow during the early stages of the reform and that the sector remained highly controlled throughout (most of) the reform period. While allowing a fair amount of institution building, authorities in, for example, Korea and Japan kept tight control over the financial sector for a long time (even though their approaches were different) in order to implement their financial allocation poli-

cies. This control took the form of administered interest rates, directed credits, and accompanying interest rate subsidies.[4] The successful examples of Korea and Japan certainly inspired and influenced China.

This section summarizes the main achievements of China's financial reform process (as of 1995) and highlights the areas where further reform is needed to achieve the goals set for the year 2000. Subsequently, financial reforms are placed against the background of the overall reform process thus far.[5]

Three Components of Financial Sector Development

During the past decade and a half of economic reforms, China's financial system has developed remarkably. Analytically, it is useful to conceive financial sector development as a balanced development of the triangle of institutions, instruments, and markets. The first element includes the establishment of banks and other financial institutions, as well as of infrastructure, such as the payments system. The instrument leg refers to the development of a range of financial instruments available to market participants to invest and trade. Development of the third component, markets, presupposes the free operation of the price mechanism across financial markets. Without price flexibility, financial markets do not mature either to support trade and investment or to conduct economic policy.

Application of this triangle to China's financial system indicates that most attention has been given to institution building. The process of market development—including liberalization of financial opera-

---

[3]See Sachs and Woo (1994). The authors argue that the divergent reform experiences of China, on the one hand, and Eastern Europe and some countries of the former Soviet Union, on the other, originate in China's beginning its reform as an agricultural economy facing normal problems of economic development, as opposed to Eastern Europe and the countries of the former Soviet Union, which started as urban and industrialized economies confronted with problems of structural adjustment.

[4]For a more detailed overview of the approach taken in Southeast Asian countries, see World Bank (1993).

[5]For publications that cover China's reform process in all sectors, see, for instance, Perkins (1988), Blejer and others (1991), Bell, Khor, and Kochhar (1993), Tseng and others (1994), and Fan and Nolan (1994).

**Box 2. China and the Northeast and Southeast Asian "Miracles": Common and
Uncommon Features in Financial Sector Development**

The successful economic development of several Northeast Asian countries (Japan, Korea, and Taiwan Province of China) and Southeast Asian countries (Hong Kong, Indonesia, Malaysia, Singapore, and Thailand) has been accompanied by a strategy of financial sector development and liberalization that shows several similarities across countries (see World Bank (1993)). As explained below, China's financial sector development shows more similarities with this "Asian strategy" than with the path adopted by Eastern European countries, the Baltic states, Russia, and the countries of the former Soviet Union, with which China shares the transition from plan to market economy.

One of the main features of the *policy strategy* adopted (at the macroeconomic and microeconomic levels) by Asian countries under review is the continuous search for a balance between macroeconomic policies that adhere to policy *fundamentals* and selective *interventionist* policies. Selective interventions have been used more frequently in Northeast Asia than in Southeast Asia. In general, whenever selective interventions have threatened macroeconomic stability, the authorities have consistently come down on the side of prudent macroeconomic management.

The financial sector is seen as *the main vehicle for interventionist policies*. The combination of prudent macroeconomic management and selective interventions has in general led to an environment conducive to savings and investment, one of the main features of the so-called miracle. Interventionist policies, almost by definition, have relied heavily on the financial sector. Such policies usually take the form of (i) mild financial repression, (ii) directed credit programs, (iii) selective credit policies, and (iv) use of development banks and specialized institutions. To achieve their policy goals, governments usually try to keep a grip on financial sector development as long as possible.

A brief comparison of the Chinese, Northeast Asian, and Southeast Asian policy approaches reveals interesting similarities and differences in a number of areas. First, with respect to *interest rate policies*, most countries in the sample have postponed interest rate liberalization for a long time (by now, rates are liberalized in all countries, with the exception of Korea, where the process is under way). Common to all countries was the adoption of a policy of mild repression of the interest rates. In most countries, real rates were most of the time positive, although at below-market clearing levels. Rates were only occasionally allowed to be negative in real terms (for example, after shocks to the economy). This policy seems to have encouraged investment, while savings were not really discouraged because rates were never negative for a long time.

China's interest rate policy history thus far is not very different from this general picture. The interest rate structure is administratively set by the authorities. Real rates have turned negative on some occasions when inflation accelerated. To safeguard the savings pattern, long-term deposit rates have been indexed on such occasions since 1988. Interest rate liberalization is now at the fore of the agenda.

Second, credit allocation by the government through *directed credit* has been common in most of the countries under review. These programs were implemented either through state-owned banks or through private banks. World Bank (1993) identifies a major difference in the performance of these programs by the Northeast Asian group, on the one hand, and most of the Southeast Asian group, on the other. In Japan and Korea, directed credit mechanisms were based on performance criteria and seem generally to have contributed to better credit allocation. Most other countries lacked strong performance-based allocation and monitoring mechanisms and therefore have been largely unsuccessful.

In China, directed credit has remained the dominant allocation tool during most of the reform because of the continued reliance on the credit plan. Mechanisms to measure performance have been absent for a long time. The present "commercialization" of the state-owned banks and the establishment of policy lending banks indicate a turn in the policy approach.

Third, *selective credit policies* have been widely used in the Asian countries under review, including programs of subsidized interest rates for housing loans (Singapore), export credit (all countries except Hong Kong), agriculture and small and medium-sized enterprises (Indonesia, Malaysia, and Thailand) and specifically targeted sectors (Japan and Korea). China has a wide range of subsidized interest rates specifically set for individual sectors of the economy. The dominance of directed credit in China leads to a situation wherein directed credit and interest subsidy are narrowly interwoven, more than in most other countries.

Fourth, *reliance on development banks and specialized institutions* has been another means for governments to achieve the goals set by their interventionist policies. Government-owned development banks were established in Indonesia, Japan, Korea, and Taiwan Province of China. They have been most successful in the Northeast Asian countries. Most of these banks have used commercial criteria to evaluate and monitor projects, and their good performance has created spillovers to the rest of the financial system. While China has relied on "specialized" banks throughout its reforms, the emergence of development banks (policy lending banks) is a recent phenomenon, and it is too early to evaluate their operating methods and performance.

Both the role given to the financial sector in economic development and the specific interventionist policies adopted have influenced the way that the financial sector has been developing and liberalizing in most of the countries involved. In general, much attention has been paid to institution building, while market development—and the concomitant liberalization—has for a long time been selective. More generally, financial liberalization has been gradual and has come at later stages in the process. Following are the most salient features of financial sector development:

• Because of their *emphasis on bank supervision and regulation,* most countries in the sample have been more successful than others in the world in supervising and regulating the financial sector to avoid solvency problems. World Bank (1993) shows that nonperforming loans have been less of a problem in Asian countries than in most other parts of the developing world. In addition, most of the countries surveyed have met or are in the process of meeting the capital adequacy standards of the Bank for International Settlements. This is the area where China is lagging the most. Bank supervision based on market principles is still in its infancy, and it is to be feared that the reform of the state-owned enterprises will open a Pandora's box of nonperforming loans.

• To be able to keep control over the financial system—to facilitate implementation of their policies—governments in most Asian countries strictly *limited competition in the financial sector* by regulating new entries in the banking system. So, while competition was limited through the regulation of interest rates and spreads, rigid restrictions on entry (for foreign banks, as well as for local entrants) also shielded the banks from new competitors. In Northeast Asia, the banking system was strictly controlled, but governments allowed the establishment of nonbank financial institutions (NBFIs), which often were given more leeway than banks to compete and attract savings. Such policies have led to some disintermediation out of the banks. So far, China has been following a path similar to the Northeast Asian countries by limiting entry into the banking system (except for the Special Economic Zones) and encouraging (or allowing) the creation of an NBFI sector. Branches of foreign banks are not permitted to conduct renminbi-based business.

• Most countries have sought ways to expand and facilitate the *access of rural areas to the formal financial system.* In most countries, the postal savings system has been very instrumental in the success of this policy. In China, where the country's size was a major challenge, the goal has been met by establishing a vast network of rural credit cooperatives, which are linked to the banking system through the Agricultural Bank. Although it is available, the postal savings system has played a relatively minor role in creating access to the banking system.

• *Capital market development* has been relatively slow in most countries under review. Several factors account for this, such as the establishment of long-term financing institutions (Japan and Thailand), which

took away the need and appetite for a corporate bond market, and the lack of government securities markets (which in itself was a consequence of sound fiscal policies), particularly in Southeast Asia. The lack of government securities markets deprived fledgling corporate bond markets from a risk-free benchmark rate. Several countries are now making great efforts to establish capital markets. In contrast, capital market development in China started early in the reform, inspired by the need to tap alternative financial sources for the Government and for the emerging collective township and village enterprises. Even though outstanding volumes and trade activity have increased sharply, the market has been hindered by the absence of an integrated payments and settlement system, a solid legislative framework, and a nationally integrated money market.

• *Money market development,* as expected, is, among others, closely linked to interest rate liberalization. As a consequence, the money market development record in the Northeast and Southeast Asian countries is mixed. Most countries recognized the importance of having a money market early in the reform stages. However, the approach has been in most cases piecemeal or selective. Many countries have one or several money market segments (treasury bills, commercial paper, certificates of deposit, or repurchase agreements) in which interest rates have been liberalized early in the process. While these markets have been operating satisfactorily, the lack of interest rate liberalization in other parts of the money market often led to the existence of a segmented market. This phenomenon has been most visible in Korea and Indonesia. Money market development in China has been lagging, owing to the lack of interest rate liberalization and an appropriate payments and settlement infrastructure.

The absence of interest rate liberalization, the importance given to forms of directed credit, the embryonic state of the money market, and the lack of large-value payments and settlement systems are factors that in one way or another have contributed to a *slow transition from direct to indirect instruments* in most countries. It is clear from this overview that, in most countries, credit ceilings and administered interest rates dominated the range of monetary policy instruments for a long time. Only the Bank of Japan never relied on directed credit and credit ceilings, but moral suasion has been a powerful instrument in that country (as in most countries in the area). By now, indirect instruments dominate in most countries. The adoption of indirect instruments in China—more particularly, open market operations—is being slowed down by the same factors (listed above) that have affected other countries in the region. The reform agenda for the near future contains such elements as interest rate liberalization, money market development, and modernization of the payments and settlement system, which will enable the People's Bank of China to increase its reliance on indirect instruments.

tions—has received the least attention, while the development of new financial instruments has been confined to the capital markets. This view implies that, during the next stages of reform, greater emphasis will have to be placed on liberalization measures, in order to complement achievements in the two other components and to prevent the financial system from becoming a bottleneck to the development of a market economy.

Institutions

Institution building started in the early reform years with the establishment of a two-tier banking system. Gradually, the People's Bank of China (PBC) was divested of all its "commercial" activities. In 1984, the PBC became the country's central bank. Central banking received a new impetus in 1995 when a new law on the PBC was enacted that gave the central bank the legal framework to operate under the leadership of the State Council in a market environment.

Concomitantly with the gradual transformation of the PBC into a genuine central bank, the instrument framework for monetary policy has evolved. Since the mid-1980s, the PBC has introduced new monetary policy instruments, such as reserve requirements and lending to the commercial banks, to support its monetary policy actions, which remained guided by the credit plan. Even though the credit plan remained the main policy instrument, its effectiveness has been decreasing since the late 1980s, mainly because its institutional coverage started lagging behind the expansion of the banking sector. In 1994, direct central bank lending to the Government was discontinued, and preparations for the adoption of an indirect monetary policy framework were begun in earnest. These decisions have signaled the start of the phasing out of the credit plan, in line with the strategy to establish a market economy.

Beginning in 1984, new banks were permitted to operate alongside the state-owned specialized banks, which at the same time were formally allowed to diversify their operations. During the second half of the 1980s, a flourishing network of nonbank financial institutions (NBFIs) emerged. Since then, a dual-track banking system has been in operation, as four specialized banks are used to implement the Government's financial policies as laid out in the credit plan, while other, new banks enjoy more freedom in their operations. The establishment of three policy lending banks in 1994 and the enactment of the commercial bank law in 1995 are meant to facilitate transformation of the four state-owned specialized banks into commercial banks. (For a definition of policy lending banks, see the subsection on "Commercialization and Expansion" in Secion III.) The new commercial bank law will also be used to introduce more order in financial sector development by separating banking from other business. Indirectly, therefore, this law will also assist in streamlining the NBFI sector, which has suffered from underregulation and lack of supervision.

Instruments

Financial instrument development has concentrated on the gradual but significant development of capital markets in China. Capital markets began to develop in 1981 when the Government of China resumed the issuance of government securities. Shortly thereafter, other types of bonds, as well as enterprise shares, appeared, even though their issuance was strictly controlled by the authorities. Since 1988, secondary markets in bonds and stocks have been allowed to operate, and their activity has further boosted capital market development. The stock exchanges of Shanghai and Shenzhen have become the exponents of China's flourishing capital market activity.

Markets

For most of the period since 1978, developments in the third pillar of financial reform—market development and liberalization—have remained in the shadow of the institution-building process. While the four state-owned specialized banks are in principle free to develop activities outside their traditional field of specialization, their lack of expertise, the continued dominance of the credit plan, and the customers' limited freedom to choose their banking relations have hampered the ability of these banks to operate competitively.

The first attempts at liberalizing the domestic financial system were undertaken in the period 1986–88, shortly after the PBC was established as a central bank. Compliance with credit quotas was relaxed, and banks were allowed to set lending rates freely within prespecified margins above the administered rates. However, inflationary developments in 1987–88 brought these liberalization efforts to a temporary halt. Since the early 1990s, banks and NBFIs have again been granted the freedom to set lending rates within prespecified margins, with the width of the margin depending on the type of institution.

The absence of nationally organized money markets—one of the salient features of China's financial sector in the early 1990s—is related to the administrative nature of interest rate setting and the lack of a modern payments and settlement infrastructure. This

Table 1. China and the Northeast and Southeast Asian "Miracles": Financial Sector Policies and Development

	Northeast Asia (Japan, Korea, and Taiwan Province of China)	Southeast Asia (Hong Kong, Indonesia, Malaysia, Singapore, and Thailand)	China
Interventionist policies using financial sector			
Mild financial repression	Applied in all countries. Rates liberalized in Japan in 1970s–80s; in Korea, still ongoing, as in Taiwan Province of China.	Applied in all countries except Hong Kong and Singapore; rates have been liberalized in Malaysia and Thailand.	Tentative attempt to liberalize rates in late 1980s was reversed. Plans are drafted to liberalize rates by the year 2000.
Directed credit programs and selective credit policies	Intensely used in Korea; not used in this form in Japan. Development banks "guided" and "stimulated" commercial banks. Most directed credit went to private sector in Japan. In Korea, a large part went to state sector. Stringent monitoring and evaluation criteria applied, particularly in Japan.	Directed credit and selective credit policies, while used in all countries except Hong Kong, do not seem to have been very successful. Monitoring and evaluation were generally weak.	Larger part of bank credit is directed under the credit plan. All directed credit goes to SOEs. Monitoring and evaluation have never been strict.
Reliance on development banks or specialized institutions	Approach adopted by Korea and Japan. In Japan, these institutions were the main vehicles for directed and selective credit policies.	Such institutions have never been very popular in most of the Southeast Asian countries, except for Indonesia and Thailand.	Until 1993, state-owned specialized banks were used to implement policies of directed and selective credit. In 1994, policy lending banks were established for this purpose.
Financial sector development and liberalization			
Emphasis on regulation and supervision	Good record in terms of nonperforming loans.	Record in terms of nonperforming loans is on average better than other developing countries'.	Bank supervision and regulation still in infancy. Supervision still geared toward compliance with credit plan. Record in terms of nonperforming loans not yet clear.
Limits on competition	Interest rates administered for a long time (see above). Other limits included restrictions on entries. NBFI sector was granted more freedom.	Similar to Northeast Asia. Less emphasis on NBFI development.	Similar to other East Asian countries; restrictions on entries. Branches of foreign banks are not permitted to conduct renminbi business. NBFI sector was granted more freedom.
Access to financial system	Postal savings system in all countries fostered savings in rural areas and among people with low incomes in urban areas.	Similar to Northeast Asia. Least developed in Thailand.	RCCs and UCCs established in early reform years to attract rural and urban savings. Postal savings system less developed.
Capital market development	Relatively slow; in Japan, among other reasons, due to existence of long-term financing institutions.	Also relatively slow, mainly because sound fiscal position never stimulated government securities market.	A striking feature of China's reforms. Government securities market started early in reform process as alternative financing source for Government.
Money market development	Mixed record. Well developed in Japan. Some segments developed in Korea (certificates of deposit, commercial paper, and repurchase agreements).	Well developed in Hong Kong and Singapore. Some segments well developed in Thailand (repurchase agreements, certificates of deposit, and commercial paper), Indonesia, and Malaysia (certificates of deposit and bankers' acceptances). Lack of development attributable to lack of short-term government securities and of interest rate liberalization.	Underdeveloped; not integrated at the national level.

lack of a nationally integrated interbank and money market has, in turn, hampered the transition to indirect instruments of monetary policy.

Market development has probably progressed the most in the external sector. The establishment of the so-called swap centers in 1986 marked the introduction of an embryo foreign exchange market in China. Until 1992–93, the turnover of this market, organized by the swap centers under the supervision of the State Administration for Exchange Control (SAEC), grew steadily. A new phase started in 1993 when the authorities decided to unify the exchange rates used in the different swap centers (the swap rates) and, therefore, to create one national foreign exchange market. This unification was achieved at the beginning of 1994. At the same time, the official rate and the swap rate were unified.

Against this background, the agenda of financial reform for the near future will clearly have to emphasize greater flexibility in interest rates, money market development, and more competition in the banking system. Reforms in these areas, which will mutually reinforce each other, will support a more efficient allocation of funds in the economy and pave the way for a more effective use of the indirect monetary policy instruments already in place and for the introduction of open market operations as the PBC's main instrument of indirect monetary policy.

Characteristics of the Overall Reform Process

As in other sectors, financial reform has not followed a rigid, comprehensive blueprint, at least not until 1992–93. Instead, it has been characterized by pragmatism and gradualism, making reform in China evolutionary rather than revolutionary. The size and diversity of the country, as well as the decentralization in the decision making introduced early in the reform process, have allowed it to adopt small-scale "laboratory approaches" and be selective in starting specific reforms.[6] As a result, the pace and degree of reform have varied greatly across regions in China, contributing to widening regional

economic disparities. The gradual, evolutionary process has also stimulated the use of an intermediate control system, combining mechanisms of the command economy with mechanisms used in market economies.

Laboratory Approach and Selectivity

From the onset of the reform process, one of the preferred and perhaps most salient techniques of the Chinese authorities has been to undertake the reforms first on an experimental basis in some localities and adopt them on a national scale after they had proved successful at the local level. Two variants of this experimental or laboratory approach are found. In some cases, the central authorities have designated one region (province or city) as the pilot for a new project, while, in other cases, as a result of the growing decentralization of decision-making processes, local authorities themselves have initiated projects that were later officially recognized by the Central Government and treated as experimental projects of national significance.

Two factors contributed to the feasibility and success of this approach. First, the sheer size of the country makes it easier for China than for smaller countries to undertake experiments at the local level that can yield significant results. In addition, and perhaps more important, labor and capital mobility was highly restricted during the first years of the reforms in China, so that local experiments could be conducted without much spillover to the rest of the country. This kind of experimentation has increasingly become more difficult to conduct because both population and capital mobility have gained momentum.

Examples of the laboratory approach in the financial sector include the opening of local interbank centers and swap centers in selected cities in 1986 and the opening of secondary markets in government securities in six cities in 1988. In both cases, other cities were allowed to follow suit after the authorities had sufficient indications that these experiments were successful.

An example of a local initiative subsequently adopted as a national initiative was the establishment of stock exchanges. The local authorities in Shanghai and Shenzhen encouraged the development of exchanges in their cities without support from the national authorities. Later, Shanghai was recognized by the Central Government as the nation's major stock exchange experiment, followed by Shenzhen, while local attempts in other cities were put on hold.

Selectivity in the reforms is closely linked to the experimental approach. From the beginning, the

---

[6]Decentralization gave local authorities the leeway to experiment. However, it has also given them the possibility to "exploit" some of the old structures and, in fact, undermine central decision making. For instance, decentralization put the local authorities in a better position to influence branches of the PBC and specialized banks in promoting local projects. On several occasions, these policies undermined the national monetary policy objectives. This undermining of policy objectives in several policy areas has certainly contributed to the cyclical swings that have typified the Chinese economy since the start of the reforms.

Chinese authorities selected certain provinces or regions to play a leading role in the reform process. The Special Economic Zones (SEZs) are the most striking examples of this approach. These zones were given the freedom to offer special (financial and other) advantages to attract foreign investors in order to promote economic growth and the opening of the Chinese economy to the outside world. The "experimental impulse" is also part of this approach. For instance, branches of foreign banks could be opened in the SEZs, even though these banks were not allowed to conduct business in renminbi. Credit quotas in the SEZs had only an indicative character, and banks were permitted more freedom in setting their lending and deposit rates than in the rest of the country.

Intermediate Control Mechanisms

Intermediate control mechanisms have been established to smooth the transition from one economic system to the other and to familiarize the economic agents with the features and mechanisms of the newly emerging system. Examples are the establishment of a two-tier pricing system (1984), the introduction of monetary policy instruments of a more indirect type (1984), the introduction of a swap market in foreign exchange retention rights to improve the use of foreign exchange (1986), the granting of more freedom to the banks in setting interest rates (1986), and the establishment of local interbank markets to encourage banks' liquidity management (1986).

Despite some obvious advantages, it can be said with hindsight that the resort to intermediate control mechanisms has also had certain drawbacks. More particularly, there is evidence that the large cyclical movements of China's economy since 1979 can be attributed to some extent to the above-cited mixture of techniques (see Khor, (1991) and Bell, Khor, and Kochhar (1993) for more details on these

issues).[7] Each time that a new wave of innovations and reform was introduced (1979, 1984, and 1992), economic activity received a major impetus. In these circumstances, the economy began to overheat, and monetary policy measures were put in the line of fire to contain the pressure. On several occasions, however, indirect instruments of monetary policy (increases in required reserves and tightening of PBC lending) did not seem sufficiently effective to contain inflation, mainly because the appropriate environment for their use was still missing. The PBC had thus to resort to administrative controls (tighter credit quotas and increases in interest rates). However, changes in these instruments are subject to approval by the State Council, which entails long decision-making lags that involve recognition of the problems and the search for consensus on the action to be taken. In the end, such a decision-making process requires more restrictive measures than would have been necessary initially. This situation contributed to the sharp downturns and hard landings that have typified macroeconomic developments in China since the early 1980s.

---

[7]It has become common practice to divide the reforms into phases. The first phase of economic reforms (1979–84) was aimed at allowing market forces to play in agriculture and nonurban industry and to open the economy to the rest of the world. The second phase (1984–88) included the establishment of a two-tier price system, the introduction of enterprise taxation, and the reform of the wage system. The introduction of a two-tier banking sector and the transformation of the PBC into a central bank also date from 1984, while swap centers for trading retained foreign exchange earnings were introduced in 1986. The period 1988–91 was characterized by retrenchment measures as a result of the acute inflationary pressures experienced in 1988. The rectification program reintroduced some price controls, and the pace of financial reforms slowed appreciably. Credit quotas were applied more tightly, and the freedom for banks to set their interest rates was scaled down. However, these were also the years in which secondary government securities markets emerged and the NBFI sector started growing. The fourth phase started in 1992 with the declaration ending the rectification program. The macroeconomic cycles (see also Section VII) do not coincide perfectly with these reform phases because of lagging effects, but both types of phases are interrelated.

III Financial Sector Development

Financial sector development has been characterized by the establishment of a two-tier banking system, followed by the significant expansion of the sector. The sector has diversified through the emergence of nonbank financial institutions (NBFIs), while banks have been allowed to despecialize. Internationalization of the banking sector has taken place only to a limited degree. More recently, the "commercialization" of the state-owned specialized banks has received a boost with the establishment of three policy lending banks and the enactment of the law on commercial banks (see Section IV).

Reforms in the financial sector can be divided into four phases, broadly coinciding with the phases mentioned in footnote 7 in Section II. The first phase covers the re-establishment of the banking system early in the reform years. The second phase starts in 1984 and includes the establishment of a genuine two-tier banking system, diversification of the financial sector, and attempts to liberalize the sector. The third phase, the rectification period (1988–91), witnessed an interruption of the liberalization and a further growth of the NBFI sector. Since 1992, in the fourth phase, several new banks have been established, policy lending banks have been introduced, and work on a legal framework for the financial sector has been undertaken in earnest.

The Role of Banks and Banking Before Economic Reform

Before 1978, the People's Bank of China (PBC) was the dominant domestic banking institution, basically serving as a "monobank" that handled most financial transactions. Two other specialized banks, the People's Construction Bank of China (PCBC) and the Bank of China (BOC), operated as special departments within the PBC. The function of the banking system was confined to facilitating the financing of the economic plan. Investment and construction funds, as well as a minimum working capital, were supplied to enterprises in the form of budgetary grants.

The PBC and its specialized departments acted mainly as cashiers, with their functions confined to the settlement of enterprises' transactions, the administration of funds for working capital and short-term investment—for the part not already covered by budgetary grants—and the collection of household savings. Thus, their intermediation function was limited.

Bank lending covered only transitory and unexpected financial requirements above the assigned quota. Bank loans were generally short term, mostly granted to finance the accumulation of stocks or the purchase of raw materials—in effect, substitutes for buyers' credits and commercial bills. Interest was charged in an attempt to encourage enterprises to use funds more effectively. Lending rates, however, were low compared with both interest rates on savings deposits and administrative costs, and priority sectors continued to benefit from preferential rates.

Re-Establishment of Banking System (1978–84)

In the early years of the reform process, China's banking system was re-established. The PBC was restored as the country's central bank, even though it continued to perform certain "commercial" activities and remained a department of the State Council. In order to improve the allocation of financial resources to specific sectors, the PCBC and the BOC started operating as independent specialized banks, the former to handle the financial activities of the construction sector and the latter foreign transactions. The Agricultural Bank of China (ABC) was established to take over the PBC's rural banking business. In addition, a network of 60,000 rural credit cooperatives (RCCs) was set up under the supervision of the ABC to provide small-scale rural banking services.

Concomitantly, the first NBFIs began to appear: the China International Trust and Investment Corporation (CITIC), under the control of the State Council, and the China Investment Bank (CIB), under the

Chart 1. Structure of Financial Sector in 1978–84

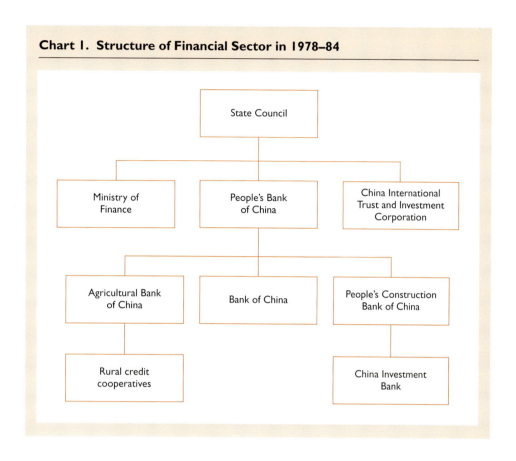

control of the PCBC. The authorities also allowed the establishment of international trust and investment companies (ITICs). These institutions raise funds from foreign sources to finance foreign-funded enterprises. In this capacity, they have been the primary source for most international bond borrowing made by China during the 1980s. Many of them were established in the coastal regions—more particularly in the Special Economic Zones (SEZs)—quite often at the provincial level. Most ITICs were established and owned by the (local) authorities. During the 1980s, the number of ITICs grew to over 100, but restructuring had by the end of the 1980s brought that number down. The structure of the banking system for the period 1978–84 is illustrated in Chart 1. While the newly established specialized banks were supposed to report to and be supervised by the PBC, they—just like the PBC—were line departments under the State Council, but at a lower ranking than the PBC.

Following a 1979 directive of the State Council, the allocation of investment funds was to shift gradually from budgetary grants to bank loans, subject to interest rates and repayment of principal. Both the PBC and the specialized banks were authorized to grant medium-term and even long-term

(five–ten years) loans for the purchase and improvement of equipment and other approved investment projects. As a consequence, the composition of funds allocated to industrial enterprises changed rapidly from 70 percent in the form of budgetary grants in 1978 to 80 percent in the form of bank lending in 1982.

Despite these changes, the banking system continued primarily to serve the limited purpose of providing the credit needed by enterprises to implement the plan for physical output within the framework of central planning. Neither the project's profitability nor the borrower's repayment ability was taken into consideration in the monitoring process.

Diversification and Innovation (1984–88)

Starting in October 1984, budgetary funds for state enterprises were further cut and replaced by bank lending. The tax reforms, which gave state enterprises full responsibility for the use of their after-tax profits, changed the destination and size of enterprise deposits: enterprises could now use their funds not only to settle approved goods transactions but also to pay wages and bonuses, as well as to finance working capital and short-term investment. In addition, the investment system was reformed to encourage enterprises to borrow from the banking system to finance projects, rather than to rely on direct grants from the state budget as in the past.

A directive of the State Council in September 1983 formally established the PBC as the country's central bank by removing its urban commercial banking activities. A fourth specialized bank, the Industrial and Commercial Bank of China (ICBC), was formed to conduct henceforth those activities. This development formally ended the transition toward a full-fledged two-tier banking system, as China became the first socialist country with a centrally planned economy to set up a two-tier banking system.

The PBC's new mandate was embodied in provisional regulations on banking that were enacted in 1986. According to those regulations, the PBC was responsible for the conduct of monetary policy and the regulation and supervision of the entire financial system, as well as of money and capital markets. The PBC became functionally equivalent to a line ministry under the State Council, which implied that all economic and financial decisions of the PBC Council—its policymaking body—needed approval by the State Council.[8]

The new mandate shifted the PBC's main objective from that of passively supplying cash and credit under the cash and credit plan to fulfilling the traditional functions of a central bank. To that end, the PBC began reorganizing itself and developing new instruments and working methods. However, the predominance of the credit plan and associated policy lending greatly reduced the PBC's ability to perform traditional central banking functions. The PBC's branch structure, like that of the specialized banks, is based on the administrative structure and hierarchy of the country, with branches at the level of the province, the prefecture and municipality, and the county. The city level takes a special position, as it is not subordinated to the provincial level and has independent planning status.

The financial sector diversified further after 1984. The establishment of the ICBC was followed in 1986 by the opening of some 1,200 urban credit cooperatives (UCCs) under ICBC supervision. Following the example and successful experience of the RCCs, the UCCs were created to serve small individually or collectively owned enterprises.

In the subsequent years, many of the measures taken in 1984 were expanded. New banks were established at the provincial level, and all banks were allowed to engage in foreign transactions in 1986. Two "universal" or "comprehensive" banks—the Bank of Communications (BOCOM), which had merged with the PBC in 1949 but remained in operation in Hong Kong, and the CITIC Industrial Bank, a wholly owned subsidiary of CITIC—were permitted to compete with the state-owned specialized banks in all forms of business.

Greater competition in the banking system was sought by reducing restrictions on the activities of the state-owned specialized banks—they were permitted to engage in lending outside their traditional domain—and increasing the banks' responsibility for their financial results. In practice, however, the operations of the specialized banks remained concentrated in their particular sector of origin. A limited number of foreign banks were allowed to open branches in the SEZs. Their business scope remained limited to foreign-trade-related operations, and they were not permitted to engage in renminbi-denominated activities.

A major innovation was the proliferation, starting in 1986, of trust and investment companies (TICs), as well as of securities houses. TICs receive government and enterprise trust deposits or entrusted deposits[9] and, particularly the larger ones, also underwrite and broker securities. Most TICs were established by the four state-owned specialized banks, while other banks, the Ministry of Finance (through its bureaus of finance), and some municipalities also own TICs. Banks initially established these TICs as vehicles to circumvent the credit quotas, but most TICs increasingly engaged in banking business, taking household deposits and granting working capital loans. In the late 1980s, the number of TICs operating throughout China peaked at 365.

The securities companies are owned, jointly or individually, by provincial governments, banks, and TICs. A small number of securities companies have been established by the Ministry of Finance and deal exclusively in government securities. Finally, other types of NBFIs proliferated in China's financial markets, such as leasing companies, insurance companies, and finance companies. The latter were formed by enterprise groups primarily to recycle intragroup funds among large industrial and commer-

---

[8]The PBC Council was composed of the Governor and five Deputy Governors of the PCB, one Vice-Minister each from the Ministry of Finance, State Planning Commission, and System Reform Commission, and the presidents of the four state-owned specialized banks and the People's Insurance Company of China.

[9]Trust deposits are invested or lent at the discretion and risk of the TIC and are thus similar to bank deposits; entrusted deposits are lent or invested at the specific instruction and risk of the depositor.

Chart 2. Structure of Financial Sector in 1984–88

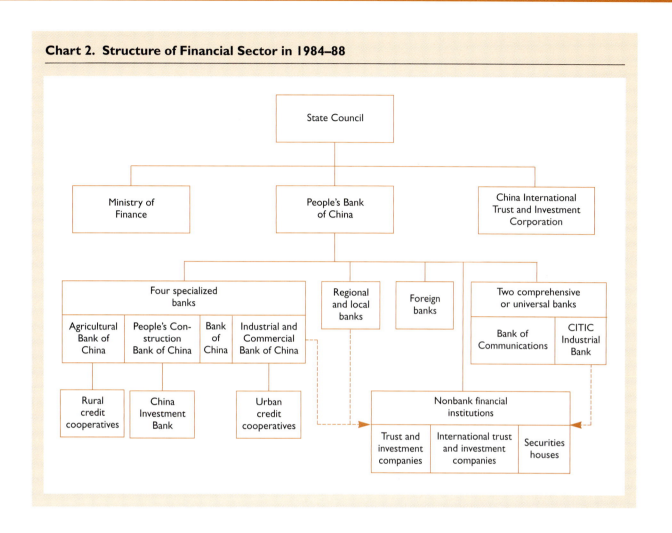

cial enterprises. The structure of the financial system in effect after the 1984 reforms is illustrated in Chart 2.

Rectification and Recentralization (1988–91)

The pace of reform in the financial sector slowed appreciably during 1988–91 because of the effects of the rectification program.[10] Considerable recentralization took place; the role of directed credit re-

gained significance (the share of the government budget in investment financing went up again); there was more uniformity in interest rates as the flexibility given the banks to set rates within prespecified margins was reduced; the specialization of the major banks was reasserted; and the authorities reverted to the previous practice of limiting enterprises' banking business to one bank only.

The same forces were felt in the NBFI sector. A reorganization of the TIC subsector became necessary in 1988 because the banks increasingly channeled part of their lending activities through their TICs, which were thus considered one of the channels through which inflation was fueled. In addition, the large number of TICs made adequate supervision by the PBC nearly impossible. The number of TICs was significantly reduced by closing or merging with the specialized banks those TICs that were established at the levels below national, provincial, and city.

Despite the rectification measures, this period was also characterized by progress in the introduction of

---

[10]The rectification program was a stabilization program introduced in the wake of a bout of inflationary pressures (by mid-1988, the 12-month inflation rate reached 30 percent). Structural reforms were given lower priority than stabilization, and administrative measures were used to supplement nascent indirect instruments of macroeconomic control. The plans for a new round of price reforms were deferred, and some earlier reforms were reversed (e.g., some price controls were reintroduced). For more details, see the "Monetary Developments" subsection of Section VII.

Box 3. Policy Lending and Policy Lending Banks

The separation of policy lending from commercial lending has become a critical issue. The leading idea behind the establishment in 1994 of three policy lending banks is to channel the flow of new policy lending through these newly created institutions. This is a significant step in the commercialization of the state-owned banks. In addition, the clear separation of commercial lending from policy lending will facilitate the implementation of indirect monetary policy, that is, liquidity management at the level of the system, rather than liquidity management at the level of individual banks or liquidity management simply to meet credit plan targets, or both.

However, the provisions of Article 41 of the Law of the People's Republic of China on Commercial Banks (1995), which stipulate that "commercial banks wholly owned by the State shall provide loans for projects approved by the State Council," seem to indicate that policy lending might not be confined to the policy lending banks (see Section IV, "Legal Underpinning for a Market-Based Financial System"). In addition, the specialized banks are still burdened by a stock of nonperforming loans generated by past policy lending, which, according to PBC estimates, amount to as much as 15 percent of their portfolio. This is an issue that the authorities will have to address in the near future.

Cleaning up the loan portfolios of the state-owned banks implies the need to define policy lending properly. Although there is no uniform definition of policy-based lending, the following five categories of policy-based loans can be identified:

- power and transport infrastructure investment loans, which can be sound financially but are generally large and have long-term repayment periods;
- fixed-asset loans designed to enhance the technology of state-owned enterprises (SOEs) included in the five-year plan, regardless of their financial health;
- loans for the development of rural areas, including the alleviation of poverty;
- working capital loans to priority SOEs, including structurally loss-making enterprises of significant national or regional political impact; and

- loans for subsidized sectors, such as education and health.

Because policy loans are meant to support the priority sectors identified in the Government's economic policies, they are mandatory. Therefore, the projects to be financed with these loans might not meet commercial banks' criteria for lending.

The outstanding stock of policy lending at the beginning of the 1990s reached about one third of the total outstanding loans extended by the banking system.

With respect to the policy lending banks, the State Development Bank will be responsible for financing key construction and infrastructure projects and strategic industries. Its coverage is quite broad as it could finance (i) highways, ports, power, and railways; (ii) basic industries, such as the steel and the chemical industries, and raw materials; (iii) emerging industries, such as the automobile and electronics industries; and (iv) other priority state projects in other sectors, including forestry and agriculture. The Import-Export Credit Bank has a narrower scope; it will provide buyers and sellers credits in support of import and export activities. The Agricultural Development Bank will become a purely policy-based lending institution, whose activities will include financing the state's procurement of agricultural products and agricultural development.

Since policy lending is a quasi-fiscal activity, the funding of the policy banks is becoming a critical issue. Heavy reliance of policy lending on central bank funding and difficulties in ascertaining the proper use of funds contributed in the past to expansionary monetary policies. Moreover, the development of interbank transactions and the commercialization of the state banks render the monitoring of specialized banks' policy-lending activities increasingly difficult. The State Development Bank is to be financed with capital provided by the Ministry of Finance and from existing funds for key construction projects, bonds issued to the public, and a portion of deposits from the PCBC. The Import-Export Credit Bank will be financed with capital from the Ministry of Finance. The Agricultural Development Bank will be financed through bonds issued to financial institutions.

---

new financial instruments and markets (see the discussion in Section V on financial markets).

Commercialization and Expansion (1992–Present)

In early 1992, the authorities declared an end to the rectification program and announced their intention to accelerate the process of reforming and opening the economy. The period since 1992 has witnessed an expansion of the banking sector and, in 1994, the establishment of three policy lending banks, designated to be the main vehicles for policy-based lending in the future (see Box 3). Policy lending can be defined as that part of bank lending that is made at the request of (or strongly encouraged by) the government to promote its economic, industrial, and sectoral policies and to assure funding for priority activities (see Box 3). Such lending may or may not be made at subsidized interest rates. The estab-

Chart 3. Structure of Financial Sector in 1994

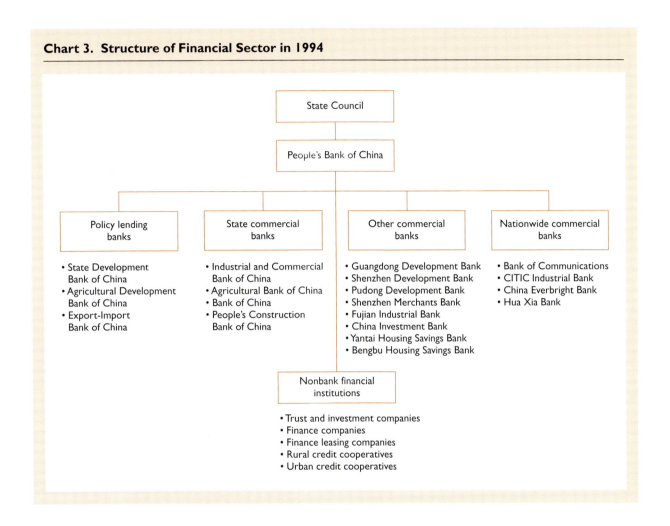

lishment of these policy lending banks was intended to pave the way to a further commercialization of the state-owned specialized banks, henceforth to be called state commercial banks.[11] Two of the newly licensed banks are "nationwide commercial banks," the new name for what were formerly called universal banks. In addition, six other commercial banks, most of them of regional significance, have been licensed, together with two "housing savings banks." Some of these regional banks, particularly those established in fast-growing areas such as Guangdong Province, Shenzhen, and Shanghai, are quickly gaining importance. In the near future, the authorities plan to transform the state commercial banks into competitive, autonomous, and self-accountable commercial entities, whose operations would be supported by an appropriate legal framework. Plans

also exist to transform the UCCs into commercial banks, which, as smaller entities, would become driving forces behind local urban development plans.

Growth in the number of TICs and securities houses has remained limited in the period since 1992. In the NBFI sector in general, the authorities contemplate the promotion of institutions providing medium- and long-term funding for investment purposes. A main goal for the authorities is to impose strict border lines between banking and other activities. For the moment, several TICs conduct banking and trust operations, and they will have to choose between becoming banks or remaining TICs (which do not conduct banking operations). Chart 3 depicts the basic structure of the financial sector in China in 1995.

Present Characteristics

After approximately 15 years of reform, the four state-owned specialized banks still dominate the fi-

---

[11]The paper tries consistently to use the term "state-owned specialized banks" for the period before 1992–93 and "state commercial banks" after 1992–93. In a few cases, it was difficult to draw this strict line.

Chart 4. Deposit Money Banks, 1985:IV–1994:III
(In percent)

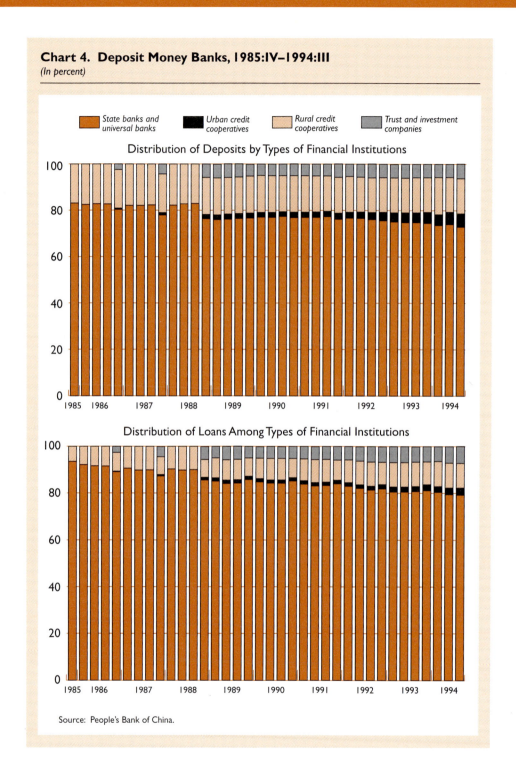

State banks and universal banks | Urban credit cooperatives | Rural credit cooperatives | Trust and investment companies

Distribution of Deposits by Types of Financial Institutions

Distribution of Loans Among Types of Financial Institutions

Source: People's Bank of China.

nancial sector. Chart 4 indicates that through the third quarter of 1994 the four state-owned special-ized banks and four universal banks still held almost 73 percent of total deposits (down from 83 percent in 1985) and 80 percent of total lending (down from 94 percent at the end of 1985). The RCCs, with about 58,000 locations, held 15 percent and 10 per-cent of deposits and loans, respectively. TICs as a group had a market share of almost 6 percent of both lending and deposits, while the UCCs, with approxi-mately 3,500 locations, accounted for about 6 per-cent of deposits and 3 percent of total sector lending.

The share of TICs and RCCs in total deposits has remained roughly constant since 1991, while the UCCs have expanded their deposit share to the detriment of the large banks. Tendencies on the lending side are slightly different because the shrinking share of the large banks has been taken in roughly equal proportions by the other types of institutions.

Despite the significant progress made in developing a banking system and the contribution made by China's banking system to the financial deepening of the country, banks in China—and, in particular, the four state-owned specialized banks—cannot be characterized as modern, efficient banking institutions. This situation is mainly due to the uneven path of past reforms, the Government's views regarding the role of banks in the reform process, and political and administrative considerations. More specifically, four major impediments to the modernization process can be distinguished.

First, during most of the period since 1978, *bank supervision and prudential control* have remained geared toward ensuring compliance with economic regulations, in particular, the fulfillment of the credit plan. Criteria and regulations that prevail in a market-oriented environment, such as bank soundness and safety and, ultimately, stability of the financial system, have not yet been integrated into the supervisory and regulatory framework by the authorities. This in part reflects the lack of a broad legal operating framework for banks during most of the reform period. At a more specific level, proper loan classification and adequate provisioning for bad loans (see below) have not yet been applied. Eliminating this regulatory and supervisory gap looms as one of the big challenges in the commercialization process of the four major banks. A lack of market-oriented supervision has also led to a situation wherein the four state-owned specialized banks de facto have become universal banks, with all the risks that this entails in an inadequately regulated environment.

Second, the four state-owned specialized banks never experienced an arm's-length *relationship with the Government*, a situation that has had several repercussions. For most of the time since their establishment, this close relationship has meant that the specialized banks had to follow conflicting mandates. Banks have increasingly been stimulated to become profit oriented, while at the same time they have had to operate under government instructions, mostly in the form of policy lending. Given the vagueness surrounding the definition offered in Box 3, it is difficult to make an accurate estimate of the share of policy loans in the banks' loan portfolio. A World Bank (1995) estimate puts policy lending in 1991 at about 67 percent of the BOC's lending,

58 percent of the PCBC's, 51 percent of the ABC's, and 18 percent of the ICBC's.

One of the main consequences of the dominance of policy lending in the banks' lending activities is the low quality of their loan portfolio. Faced with the pressure of policy lending, the state-owned specialized banks have failed to adopt modern management techniques such as asset/liability management, loan risk assessment, and loan monitoring. Some estimates put the aggregate amount of nonperforming loans of the state-owned specialized banks at roughly 15 percent of their total outstanding loans.

Third, the *accounting and management information systems* are still largely designed to ensure compliance with administrative guidelines under the credit plan, rather than to deliver a picture of the banks' financial position or information relevant for making management decisions. The lack of modern accounting techniques delays the introduction of modern asset-liability management techniques, as well as of macroeconomic liquidity management by the PBC (see Section VII). The delay in the introduction is also related to the fourth impediment to modernization, as the present structure of the banks is not conducive to integrated management.

Fourth, the high degree of *decentralization of the branch structure* is another impediment to adopting modern bank management techniques. The status of the bank branches in China has always been an interesting issue. Branches in China enjoy such a high level of autonomy that they do not fit the definition of a branch as understood in industrialized countries. At the origin of the branches' unique position is the way in which the PBC and the four state-owned specialized banks were formed. At the separation of their functions (in the early 1980s), the PBC received the lion's share of the total "headquarters" institution, leaving each of the four specialized banks the task of building a headquarters unit. This job has proven to be difficult because the branches were well established and well rooted in the local political structures. In addition, the early reform years were marked by a mood of economic decentralization that made the establishment of strong headquarters tantamount to going against the reform tide. It is now difficult to bring the branches under the headquarters' direction and control, and, as a consequence, it is not an easy task to introduce principles such as liquidity management and asset/liability management in supersized banks with between 28,000 (PCBC) and 56,000 (ABC) branches. For its part, the lack of integrated liquidity management delays the introduction of indirect monetary policy, which, by definition, is based on monitoring and guiding aggregate liquidity developments in the financial system.

IV Legal Underpinning for a Market-Based Financial System

Until 1995, the existence and operations of the People's Bank of China (PBC) were based upon provisional regulations promulgated in 1986. The four state-owned specialized banks and the universal banks each operated on the basis of specific charters. The new reform strategy adopted by the Third Plenum recognized the need for a strong legal framework to underpin the orderly growth of the financial system. By the end of 1993, four draft financial laws were submitted to the State Council: the Law of the People's Republic of China on the People's Bank of China, the Law of the People's Republic of China on Commercial Banks, the Negotiable Instrument Law of the People's Republic of China, and the Insurance Law of the People's Republic of China. These laws were all enacted in 1995. Since 1993, the PBC has also promulgated several regulations to streamline banking operations and strengthen its supervision of the financial sector. Furthermore, other laws, such as that on nonbank financial institutions (NBFIs), are still in preparation. This section discusses the main features of the PBC law (passed in March 1995) and of the commercial bank law (passed in June 1995); these laws can be considered the keystones for the further development of the financial system in a market-based economy.

Establishment of a Legal Framework for the Central Bank

Ten years after the establishment of the PBC as China's central bank in 1984, the People's Congress enacted a law giving the central bank the power to perform central bank functions. The preceding reform years had increasingly shown the need for an autonomous entity with the power to regulate the financial system and conduct monetary policy.

At the time that the Chinese authorities were reassessing the legal framework for the central bank, the case for giving central banks a high degree of independence from the political authorities was being made convincingly worldwide, as illustrated, inter alia, by the Statute of the European System of Central Banks and the European Central Bank (1993). However, the organization, role, and functions of the insti-

tution in charge of monetary policy in China have to be assessed in light of Article 2 of the PBC law, which establishes the leadership of the State Council in the formulation and implementation of monetary policy.

Autonomy of the Central Bank

Developments in central bank legislation in several countries suggest that the establishment of a balance between central bank autonomy and the coordination of monetary and other economic policies is a crucial issue. Traditionally, central banks have been granted formal independence, but governments have retained enough power to influence important decisions. More recently, legislation has moved in the direction of granting full autonomy to the central bank in monetary matters, under the assumption that a strong and independent central bank would be in a better position to maintain price stability.[12]

The Chinese authorities were facing the dilemma of having to give up certain aspects of the traditional political structure to allow the central bank more autonomy versus retaining the present decision-making structure (centralized in the State Council and based on consensus building), within which the PBC

---

[12]For instance, the Law of the Autonomy of the Banco de España and the Statute de la Banque de France include similar provisions in this respect: "The Bank is an institution under public law with its own legal personality and full public and private legal capacity. It shall pursue its activities and fulfill its objectives with autonomy from the administration, carrying out its functions as specified in this law and other legislation" (Article 1). Also, Article 12 of the Federal Bank Act in Germany states that the Bundesbank "shall be independent of instructions by the federal Government in the exercise of the authority granted to it by this Act." Similar arrangements had been enshrined in the Statute of the European System of Central Banks and the European Central Bank adopted under the Maastricht Treaty. This trend is also present in Latin America: in Chile, the Central Bank is an autonomous institution, with its own resources; in Mexico, the central bank was granted constitutional status and provided with full autonomy in its functions and administration; in Argentina, the Central Bank is granted the highest degree of autonomy under Argentine law. However, this is not the case in some Asian countries, such as Thailand, where the Minister of Finance has charge and control of the execution of the Central Bank Act. Moreover, the general supervision of the affairs of the Bank of Thailand is vested in the Minister of Finance.

could fulfill its mission in a market-based environment. The critical questions were therefore, what type of agency should the PBC become, and how independent should it be from the State Council to perform these functions? It was evident from the outset that, although lessons could be drawn from recent developments in central bank legislation elsewhere, it would be difficult to copy the concept of an autonomous central bank in China at that time. In the Chinese political and institutional setting, an autonomous entity separate from the state would have been inconceivable. Creating such an institution would have amounted to establishing an entity separate from the State Council without any authority, because the state, as represented by the State Council, is the source of all authority.

The solution to the dilemma is reflected in the combination of the provisions of Articles 2 and 7 of the PBC law. Article 2 establishes an agency under the leadership of the State Council, which entrusts this agency with a high level of independence from all other levels of government. Article 7 stipulates that in the exercise of its functions the PBC shall be "free from intervention by local governments, or other administrative organs at all levels, public organizations or individuals."

The Central Bank as Legal Entity

A related issue is the legal status of the PBC. A central bank must be a legal entity because it must be able to act as an independent legal person, that is, to have paid-up capital, to own assets, to enter into contracts, and to sue and be sued. A corollary to this issue is that of budgetary autonomy, which enables a central bank to undertake operations without having to rely on resources from the government budget.

Since its establishment in 1984, the PBC had been a line department under the State Council. The 1995 PBC law is innovative in that it gives the central bank all the features of a legal entity, although it does not refer to the notion as such. Under Article 8, the PBC is endowed with paid-up capital and, in accordance with the provisions of Article 40, has to complete an annual balance sheet and a profit-and-loss account, to be published in an annual report. Moreover, Articles 37 and 38 confer a reasonable degree of budgetary independence on the PBC.

The assertion in Article 38 that "losses sustained by the PBC shall be offset by state allocations" is important because it will insulate monetary policy from losses that could be generated by quasi-fiscal activities undertaken by the PBC. The unusual provision that the PBC's budget is to be incorporated into the central government budget and subject to verification by the State Council reflects the present-day reality in China. However, independence of the PBC

from all other levels of Government is reinforced by the PBC's independent control over its budget.

The leadership of the State Council is also demonstrated by its power to nominate the Governor and Deputy Governors of the PBC. The absence of a management board, in turn, reinforces the authority of the Governor in the day-to-day management of the PBC and, in fact, allows for a more direct participation of the State Council in the decision-making process of the PBC because there is no intermediary body between the Governor and the State Council.

Primary Objective of the Central Bank

At the heart of effective central bank autonomy is a clear definition of the primary objective. The past practice of giving central banks multiple objectives—promoting economic growth, full employment, and price stability—has generated policy conflicts and made proper assessment of the central bank's performance difficult. These insights have recently led to a different approach whereby central banks are endowed with only one principal objective, the promotion and maintenance of price stability.

Among recent central bank legislation, the Statute of the European System of Central Banks and the European Central Bank is a clear example of establishing price stability as the primary objective of a central bank. The wording of Article 3 of the PBC law follows closely these recent developments as it stipulates that "the aim of monetary policies is to maintain the stability of the value of currency and thereby promote economic growth." The relationship drawn between economic growth and price stability clearly acknowledges the assumption that the best way central banks can promote economic growth in the longer term is by ensuring price stability. In this respect, the PBC law contrasts with broader definitions of the primary objective for the central bank in some neighboring countries, such as Japan, Korea, and Malaysia.[13]

The PBC law makes no reference to the external stability of the currency. This is not unusual in modern central bank legislation, although in some coun-

---

[13]The Bank of Japan's objectives, as detailed in Article 1.1 of its central bank law, for instance, include not only "the regulation of the currency" but also "the control and facilitation of credit and finance, and the maintenance and fostering of the credit system, pursuant to the national policy, in order that the general economic activities of the nation might adequately be enhanced." In the case of Korea, the primary purposes of the central bank are, according to Article 3 of its central banking law, "to maintain the stability of the value of the money in the interest of national economic progress, and further economic growth and efficient utilization of national resources by the sound operations and functional improvement of the nation's banking and credit system." In Malaysia, besides the promotion of monetary stability and sound financial structure, the principal objective of the central bank is to influence the credit situation to the advantage of the federation.

tries the relevant law refers to domestic and external stability.[14] The law is also silent on the responsibility for defining the exchange rate arrangements. This omission is consistent with legislation in other Asian countries,[15] although there is a tendency in modern central bank legislation to confer such responsibility on the government.[16]

Responsibility for Formulating and Implementing Monetary Policy

Effective monetary policy also requires operational autonomy, that is, the responsibility for formulating and implementing monetary policy. Recent developments in central bank legislation point to the appropriateness of increased autonomy in the formulation and implementation of monetary policy. However, there are also countries where responsibility is shared between the central bank and the government, with specific provisions made to facilitate the coordination of monetary policy with fiscal and other economic policies, and to settle conflicts.[17]

---

[14]Among the members of the European Union, this is the case in Austria and Portugal.

[15]In Japan, the central bank law is silent on the role of the central bank in exchange rate policy. In practice, the Minister of Finance, in close contact with the Bank of Japan, decides on exchange rate policy and instructs the Bank to intervene to prevent extreme fluctuations. In Korea, Article 43 of the central bank law explicitly indicates that the Government decides on the exchange regime, as the Bank of Korea reports annually on the "Government's exchange rate policies." The same situation applies in Malaysia, where Article 19 of the relevant law states that "the parity of the ringgit shall be determined by the Minister on the recommendation of the Bank."

[16]For instance, among the central banks of the European Union, only the central bank of Sweden has direct responsibility for defining the exchange regime. In some countries (Spain and Portugal), the central bank is consulted; in other countries (Finland), the central bank proposes to the government, or, as in Austria, it cooperates with the government. In all the other European Union countries, the exchange rate regime is the sole responsibility of the government.

[17]Recent European experience provides examples of greater autonomy for central banks. In Spain, coordination is assured by the participation without vote of the Director-General of the Treasury and Financial Policy and the Economy and Finance Minister in central bank board sessions; a similar provision appears in the French law. In other cases, the law regulates directly the solution of potential disagreements. The Bank of Canada Act provides that the Minister of Finance and the Governor shall consult regularly. In case of differences of opinion on monetary policy, the Minister may, after consultation with the Governor and with the approval of the Governor in Council, give to the Governor a written directive, with which the Bank of Canada shall comply. In a similar vein, the Reserve Bank of New Zealand Act requires the Reserve Bank to agree with the Minister of Finance on target price increases. In some Asian countries, central bank autonomy remains more limited. In Japan for instance, although the central bank board has the sole authority over interest rate policies, the Minister of Finance can intervene if deemed necessary. In Korea, the Government may also formulate monetary and credit policies but shall consult with the central bank board.

Under the new law, the PBC's operational autonomy is not complete. Article 2 stipulates that "the People's Bank of China shall formulate and implement monetary policies and exercise supervision and control over the financial industry under the leadership of the State Council." This leadership is reinforced by the establishment of a monetary policy committee, placed fully under the supervision of the State Council, which is also in charge of prescribing its functions, organization, and working procedures. The establishment of the monetary policy committee can help establish the autonomy of monetary policy within the State Council and thus solidify the credibility of China's monetary policy. The PBC, however, is fully responsible for implementing monetary policy measures.

Functions of the Central Bank

The functions of the PBC used to be confined to managing the issue of currency, which could involve quasi-fiscal activities, and implementing the credit plan. However, the changing institutional structure of the financial system and the development of a market-based economy called for new functions for the PBC.

Supervision of financial institutions is a function that has assumed greater importance in many countries with the liberalization of financial systems and the development of markets. There is no definite answer as to whether the central bank or another agency should undertake this function; there are pros and cons to separating monetary policy and prudential control, and country experiences provide a wide spectrum of successful solutions to the problem.[18]

The decision in China has been to give the PBC a large and direct responsibility in supervising the financial system. Article 4 of the PBC law specifies the role of the PBC in supervising and controlling financial institutions and the financial market, and Chapter V of the law deals entirely with the supervision of financial institutions, focusing on the health of individual institutions and the financial system as a whole. The law establishes the supervisory authority of the PBC over the state commercial banks and gives the PBC all means needed for effective supervision.

---

[18]In Canada and Germany, banking supervision is vested in a separate agency, although the Bundesbank in Germany assists the Supervisory Office in many ways. In the United States and Japan, the central banks share formal responsibilities. Meanwhile, in France, the United Kingdom, New Zealand, and Korea, for instance, the central bank has prime responsibility. The Statute of the European System of Central Banks and the European Central Bank foresees only a limited role for the central bank in the area of prudential control, as the national authorities are to remain the main players in this area, and a certain coordinating role is envisaged for the European Central Bank.

The decision to combine monetary policy and prudential control in the PBC is appropriate for China, as it is for other transition economies. The evidence is mounting in these countries that monetary stability can be seriously affected by the operations of insolvent banks. Furthermore, the need to strengthen the PBC's leadership over the state commercial banks suggested that this objective could be better achieved by vesting the two functions in one and the same agency.

Instruments of Monetary Policy

Because operating procedures for the conduct of monetary policy evolve in line with market developments, the listing of instruments in a central bank law should be general, with a minimum of specifications, to allow the central bank the greatest flexibility possible in conducting monetary policy.

In the case of China, moreover, the drafting of the law had to take into account the transitional period that the country was going through, as direct instruments were being gradually phased out and indirect instruments were not yet fully operational. In the transition to market-based monetary policy, the central bank law had to allow the continuation of direct controls while also giving a clear signal with respect to the direction in which the authorities wanted to go. The list of monetary instruments in Article 22 of the PBC law reflects this shift from direct to indirect monetary management. All the instruments listed belong to the category of indirect instruments, including the PBC's buying and selling of government securities in open market operations and its use of reserve requirements. Also, under Article 27, the PBC can determine the amount, interest rate, and duration of its lending to financial institutions without previous approval from the State Council.[19] This important provision empowers the PBC to engage in active interest rate management—a clear break with past practice, in which interest rate changes had to be approved by the State Council. Meanwhile, direct controls can be retained under Article 22(6), which allows the use of any instruments other than those specifically listed, provided that they are defined by the State Council.

Because Article 25 prohibits overdraft facilities, PBC credit to the banks can take the form of rediscount or loans only, that is, credit with a predeter-

mined maturity. However, the law does not formally prohibit uncollateralized lending. Although the recent policy of the PBC has been to increase the importance of collateralized lending through the rediscount window, the bulk of the PBC's credit to the banks still takes the form of uncollateralized lending. The phasing out of such lending may take a long time, as it is related to bank reform in general and the development of proper collateral in particular.

Regional Participation in Monetary Policy

The complexity and geographical size of China raised the question of regional participation in the formulation or implementation of monetary policy. Germany and the United States provide two models of a centralized organization with regional participation.[20] In the case of China, the involvement of the local governments in formulating or implementing monetary policy was a sensitive issue. Decentralization of economic decision making in the early reform years had shifted a share of economic power from the center to local governments. At times, this shift proved to be a major hindrance to effective implementation of monetary policy, as local authorities demanded additional borrowing from the local PBC branches, thereby exceeding the quota assigned under the credit plan.

In order to preserve the uniformity of monetary policy and to remove a major source of conflict between local and national interests, the PBC law makes no mention of the participation of local governments in the formulation of monetary policy. On the contrary, Article 7 explicitly rules out provincial participation in the implementation.

The relation between the PBC headquarters and its branches was another sensitive issue to consider

---

[19]The 1994 decision to phase out PBC direct credit to the Government is now enshrined in Article 28 of the PBC law. This provision is similar to those in the laws of the central banks that enjoy the highest degree of autonomy. In the case of China, it is also important that this prohibition against lending to the Government is extended to all levels of government. This disposition, together with the dispositions enhancing the authority of the PBC over its branches, will facilitate the phasing out of (autonomous) lending by PBC branches to local governments.

[20]Soon after World War II, a central banking system was set up in Germany consisting of legally independent regional central banks (the "Land Central Banks"), established by the State Government of each Land, and a joint, "umbrella-type" subsidiary of the Land Central Banks (the "Bank deutsche Länder"). The latter issued notes and performed other central bank functions on behalf of the regional institutions. The present Deutsche Bundesbank was established in 1957 through the amalgamation of the Land Central Banks and the Bank deutsche Länder. The Land Central Banks lost their independent legal status and became "main offices" of the Deutsche Bundesbank. However, the establishment of a centralized central bank did not preclude a permanent regional participation, as the Central Bank Council includes all the presidents of the Land Central Banks.

The United States offers a model of a rotating provincial representation. The presidents of the Federal Reserve Banks—except for the President of the Federal Reserve Bank of New York, who is a permanent member—serve one-year terms on a rotating basis as members of the Federal Open Market Committee. In Germany, therefore, regional participation takes place at the level of the Central Bank Council, whereas in the United States it takes place at the level of the Federal Open Market Committee.

in drafting the law. The PBC's branch network has had a significant role in implementing the credit plan; however, with the diminishing importance of the credit plan, the importance of the PBC network in implementing monetary and credit policies is also bound to diminish. Therefore, the move toward indirect monetary management could be seized to redesign and reduce the PBC's branch network. In light of the historical reality that local branches depend as much on local authorities as on the PBC headquarters (see Huang (1994)), the PBC's authority over its branch network was not evident; the law had explicitly to give PBC headquarters the autonomy to decide on the number, location, and functions of its branches. Article 12 establishes the clear leadership of the PBC headquarters over its branches, which implies a break with past practice.

Summary: How Much Autonomy for the PBC?

Although the PBC law establishes a fair degree of operational autonomy, the PBC remains an institution under the leadership of the State Council. This leadership encompasses the formulation and implementation of monetary policy; the nomination of the Governor and Deputy Governors of the PBC (under Article 9); the operations of the monetary policy committee (under Article 11); and the supervision of the PBC budget (under Article 37).

The law reveals a deep understanding of the technicalities, implications, and constraints involved in conducting monetary policy in a market environment. The PBC is vested with all the functions of a modern central bank, including the conduct of monetary policy; the issue of the currency; the centralization and administration of the foreign exchange reserves of the country;[21] the supervision of financial institutions and financial markets; and oversight of payments and clearing systems. It is also important that a measure of accountability is introduced in Article 40, which obligates the PBC to publish an annual report with the relevant financial statements.

The new PBC law should be viewed as a further step in developing China's legal system and in developing a central bank with a strong ability to implement effective monetary policy. The new law, however, remains a compromise, reflecting new trends in central banking worldwide, as well as China's present stage of constitutional and legal development, in which the power is controlled by the

Party and vested in the State Council. In these circumstances, greater independence from these sources of authority would most likely reduce the law's effectiveness. As such, the law falls short of western concepts of central bank autonomy, but it creates a central bank with a well-defined primary objective and a higher degree of autonomy than in some neighboring countries.

In the present circumstances, the best assurance that the primary objective of the PBC—as set forth in Article 3, "to maintain the stability of the value of the currency and thereby promote economic growth"—will have to come from the Government's resolve to fight inflation. Finally, the route followed in adopting the PBC law illustrates the pragmatism of the Chinese authorities in the financial reform process. In many respects, the law does not break new ground; it builds on evolving practices and reflects the consensus built on the many policy issues that it raised.

The Commercial Bank Law

Following the March 1995 passage of the central banking law, the People's Congress enacted the Law of the People's Republic of China on Commercial Banks on May 11, 1995. The law, which aims to transform major domestic commercial banks into independent commercial entities, marks a further step in building a strong, comprehensive, and relatively independent banking system.

A Two-Tier Commercial Banking System

The commercial bank law establishes a de facto two-tier commercial banking system comprising (i) commercial banks, subject to prudential ratios and other international standards of portfolio risk and profitability, and under the supervision of the PBC, and (ii) the three policy lending banks, which are not subject to this law but whose operations are guided by individual charters. As indicated in Section III, separate legislation is in the making for NBFIs, such as trust and investment companies (TICs) and securities companies.

As set out in Article 2, the law applies to commercial banks, that is, corporate persons established for handling such operations as accepting deposits from the public, providing loans, and handling settlements. Article 13 clarifies that this definition includes urban and rural cooperative banks, for which the minimum required capital is lower. The law also applies to foreign-owned commercial banks, Sino-foreign joint-venture commercial banks, and subsidiaries of foreign commercial banks. As explained in Article 4, a central feature of the new law is that

---

[21]Until recently, part of the country's foreign exchange reserves were held by the Bank of China. Management of the other part was in the hands of the State Administration for Exchange Control (SAEC), which, until 1994, reported directly to the State Council. Since 1994, the SAEC has operated under the leadership of the PBC (see Section VIII).

commercial banks shall operate independently, bear risks on their own, and take responsibility for their own profits and losses. Also, no organization or individual will be allowed to interfere with commercial bank operations.

Reinforcement of the PBC's Authority

Under Article 11, the PBC is responsible for licensing new commercial banks. Moreover, as provided for under Article 12, the law concedes much discretion to the PBC in examining applications for the establishment of a commercial bank, authorizing it to consider the state of economic development and the situation of competition among banks. However, commercial banks wholly owned by the state (the four state commercial banks) are under the direct supervision of the State Council. The leadership of the State Council over the state commercial banks is made clear in Article 41, which stipulates that they can be called to support state policies; losses incurred from providing such loans shall also be assumed by the state.

The commercial bank law is also designed to bolster the control—already enshrined in the PBC law—of the PBC over the banking sector. Under Article 38, the PBC is responsible for setting credit levels that the banks cannot exceed. Specific financial ratios are also defined in the law, such as the loan-to-deposit ratio (currently, commercial banks are allowed to lend out 75 percent of the total value of their deposits) and exposure limits (loans to a same borrower shall not exceed 10 percent of total capital). The law establishes transitional arrangements for the four state commercial banks to be adopted by the State Council.

Separation of Banking and Nonbanking Activities

According to the provisions of Article 43, commercial banks are no longer allowed to invest in NBFIs (such as TICs or security companies) or in nonfinancial enterprises. In an effort to make banks concentrate on lending to enterprises, the law establishes a "China wall" between commercial banking operations and other operations that are deemed to be more volatile and speculative.

These provisions are reinforced by Article 46, which prohibits the use of interbank lending to extend fixed-asset loans. Interbank lending should be confined to cover settlement deficiencies and to bridge temporary liquidity shortages. These dispositions, although they may be difficult to enforce, aim at limiting investment in fixed assets, which contributed to the country's high inflation rate in recent years.

Enhancing Financial Discipline

The provisions of Article 48 are intended to improve financial discipline in state-owned enterprises. It stipulates that enterprises can open only one basic account with a single commercial bank. This provision intends to reduce the number of fraud cases by preventing enterprises from moving cash among different banks for nonapproved purposes.

Summary

The new commercial bank law is an important step toward designing a framework within which the financial sector can and should develop. The law delineates the activities of both the banking system and the nonbank financial sector. Overlapping activities—and the accompanying existence of a gray area between banks and NBFIs—have long been a weakness of China's financial system. Consistent with the law on the PBC, this law obliges commercial banks to comply with the PBC's supervision and prudential control, thereby enforcing the central bank's position as regulator of the financial system.[22] Equally important are the provisions of Article 22 that make each commercial bank, as a legal entity, responsible for the liabilities of all its branches. This provision is intended to mark a clear break with past practice, which permitted branches to act like independent units.

However, several provisions in the law will, by necessity, be temporary because they reflect—and will affect—current problems and Chinese realities. Thus, revisions might be needed during the next stages of the reform. For instance, the provision in Article 48 that enterprises should have their accounts in one bank is understandable in light of current fraudulent actions. However, this provision may over time stifle competition among banks. The law also provides a special position to the state commercial banks in that they "should provide loans for special projects approved by the State Council." This provision and the corresponding obligation of the Government to make restitutions for all losses incurred through such mandated loans is meant to protect these banks from irregular pressure from local authorities, but it may also prolong the granting of policy loans through these institutions. If this were to happen, the process of commercializing these banks will be hampered, which will affect the degree of competition in the banking system.

---

[22]As mentioned in Section III, during most of the reform since 1984, the four state-owned specialized banks and the PBC were politically responsible in the same way to the State Council, even though the PBC was given some supervisory powers over the specialized banks.

V Development of Money and Capital Markets

While money market development has remained slow in the first decade and a half of reforms, capital market development has become one of the most salient parts of financial development in China. The approach applied to several other sectors of the economy—small-scale experimentation, gradual relaxation of controls, and decentralization of responsibility—has also been used in this area.

Capital market development has mainly been concentrated in and borne by the government securities market. The promotion of government bond markets in China, at least in the initial years, was primarily a means of tapping and guiding available financial resources, complementary to the credit plan. More particularly, growing central government deficits as a result of policy decentralization in the first reform years forced the Government to search for financial resources other than central bank credit. The role of the government securities market as an alternative to the credit plan was reflected, among other things, in the mandatory character of the sales. Gradually, the government securities market has acquired more features of a real market without, however, entirely losing its administered character.

Other debt instruments were allowed shortly after the first issues of government securities. Enterprise shares, corporate bonds, and financial bonds (issued by banks) were first issued in the period 1982–84 while certificates of deposits appeared in 1988. Even though the volume of outstanding nongovernment debt has been growing (Chart 5), debt instruments issued by the Central Government and government agencies still represented more than 50 percent of the total at the end of 1992. Issue procedures for debt instruments other than from the Central Government showed that those instruments also complemented the credit plan, as the issues were strictly regulated by quota to ensure consistency with the plan.

Money Markets

Money markets have been slow to develop in China. The interbank market is still the main component of the money market. By 1993, a repurchase market had emerged, but this market is still relatively underdeveloped.[23] Other market segments, such as a treasury bill market, do not yet exist.

The need for intrabank and interbank transactions emerged soon after the start of the reforms, when banks were allowed to grant credit autonomously. The predecessor of interbank activities was a type of intrabank market created by the Agricultural Bank of China (ABC) in the city of When Zhou. This market allowed branches and subbranches of the bank to lend to and borrow from each other. Soon, branches of other banks in the city were included (Girardin (1995)).

In 1984–85, the first *information centers* made their appearance in some major cities, such as Beijing, Shanghai, and Guangzhou, thereby introducing the concept of an interbank market. At the origin of their appearance was the tight monetary policy stance of the People's Bank of China (PBC), which led to severe shortages of funds in some regions and excess funds in others. Even though these centers could not bridge interregional differences, they could at least balance the flows within regions.

These information centers were either the PBC branches themselves, PBC-sponsored agencies, or agencies jointly sponsored by the PBC and state-owned specialized banks. The centers received bids and offers for funds from bank branches and nonbank financial institutions (NBFIs). The majority of these transactions were unsecured. Initially, transfers were based on the centers' temporarily releasing banks' excess deposits at the PBC or by using permitted but unutilized credit lines (De Wulf and Goldsbrough (1986), p. 229).

During the first years, this embryo interbank market grew slowly, but during the 1987–88 boom years interbank operations increased rapidly. As the market conditions—and particularly the interest rates— were partially unregulated, interest rates started

---

[23]Government bonds are the underlying instruments of these repurchase agreements. Turnover was ¥ 1,832.7 million in December 1994, which is approximately one fourth of the turnover in the secondary government securities market in the same month (World Bank (1995), p. 19).

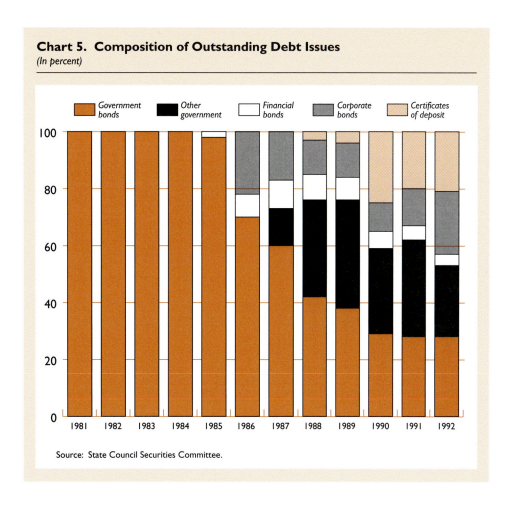

Chart 5. Composition of Outstanding Debt Issues
(In percent)

Government bonds · Other government · Financial bonds · Corporate bonds · Certificates of deposit

Source: State Council Securities Committee.

soaring and diverging widely among regions. Funds were systematically attracted by high-growth regions, where they were often used for speculative real estate projects. In addition, some malpractices started developing, such as short-term borrowing to fund long-term lending. Faced with this situation, the PBC started regulating the market. A "reference rate," around which the interbank market rate could fluctuate within a 30 percent margin, was introduced, and the Provisional Measures on the Management of Interbank Business were promulgated in 1990, aimed at standardizing and centralizing interbank market activity.

As interbank market activity grew, it also began to diversify. The number of information centers (called financing centers) grew steadily to cover most of China, with 44 centers operating in 1994.[24] However, the market remained segmented as these centers were regionally oriented. For a long time, transactions among regional centers were rare because of

technical problems (lack of a fast and reliable payments and settlement system) and political problems (the local authorities did not want the funds to flow out of their jurisdictions and therefore put restrictions on the outflows).[25] Gradually, bank branches and NBFIs also started conducting transactions with each other directly (via telephone or fax), bypassing the information centers. This direct method for conducting transactions, used mainly for short-dated transactions (for a few days to one month), is known as the intangible or invisible market, whereas the market through the information centers is known as the tangible or visible market. Maturities in the latter market are usually longer, of up to even three years.

In the period 1992–93, the interbank market started growing dramatically. In 1993, lending increased fourfold and borrowing sixfold over the pre-

---

[24]Among these 44, 6 centers (Shanghai, Wuhan, Beijing/Tianjing, Shenyang, Xian, and Chongqing) had a regional significance.

[25]Thus, from a nationwide point of view, the interbank market could not play a redistributive role. Redistribution of funds between banks (or regions) with excess liquidity and those with shortages actually was done through the PBC on the basis of its lending to the banks and its reserve requirements (see Section VII).

Table 2.   Structure of the Financial System
(In billions of yuan; end of period)

	1985	1986	1987	1988	1989	1990	1991	1992	1993	1994 Sept.
Liabilities	749.0	996.3	1,196.0	1,405.0	1,667.0	2,114.0	2,611.0	3,164.0	4,538.0	5,424.0
Total deposits	429.0	576.5	735.6	874.7	1,041.0	1,360.0	1,747.0	2,313.0	2,871.0	3,491.0
Specialized and commercial banks	356.0	463.5	573.9	668.6	798.3	1,046.0	1,330.0	1,748.0	2,140.0	2,544.0
Urban credit cooperatives	—	3.0	7.6	15.7	22.1	31.0	44.8	82.9	134.0	198.8
Rural credit cooperatives	72.5	96.2	122.5	140.0	167.0	214.5	270.9	347.2	429.7	530.1
Trust and investment companies	—	13.7	31.6	50.5	53.3	69.0	100.8	133.8	167.3	218.9
Interbank borrowing	3.3	11.8	15.2	15.7	16.8	24.9	42.8	76.3	462.0	737.2
Specialized and commercial banks	—	0.1	0.7	1.3	1.5	1.4	1.4	2.8	378.1	647.6
Urban credit cooperatives	—	—	—	—	—	—	—	—	22.4	21.7
Rural credit cooperatives	3.3	4.2	3.8	3.6	3.8	4.2	5.1	6.1	6.0	7.5
Trust and investment companies	—	7.5	10.7	10.8	11.5	19.3	36.3	67.4	55.5	60.3
PBC borrowing	225.0	268.9	276.2	337.5	421.4	511.5	594.6	675.2	964.8	955.7
Specialized and commercial banks	225.0	268.4	275.0	336.1	420.2	508.3	590.6	671.0	961.3	952.8
Urban credit cooperatives	—	—	—	—	—	—	—	—	—	—
Rural credit cooperatives	—	—	—	—	—	—	—	—	—	—
Trust and investment companies	—	0.5	1.2	1.4	1.2	3.2	4.0	4.2	3.5	2.9
Owned funds	65.3	74.1	81.4	91.4	91.4	111.5	102.3	154.3	226.9	246.6
Specialized and commercial banks	65.3	74.1	81.5	91.4	91.4	111.5	102.3	154.3	171.9	191.2
Urban credit cooperatives	—	—	—	—	—	—	—	—	—	—
Rural credit cooperatives	—	—	—	—	—	—	—	—	46.6	45.4
Trust and investment companies	—	—	—	—	—	—	—	—	8.4	10.1
Other, net	26.4	65.1	87.9	85.7	97.2	105.4	124.7	−54.4	13.2	−6.5
Specialized and commercial banks	22.0	51.5	62.7	56.7	66.8	74.1	96.0	−97.8	−54.4	−117.0
Urban credit cooperatives	—	0.2	1.6	3.3	4.8	4.8	10.2	24.7	23.1	43.2
Rural credit cooperatives	4.4	5.8	1.0	5.3	4.6	−0.2	−3.6	−0.4	16.3	6.5
Trust and investment companies	—	7.5	13.6	20.5	21.0	26.7	22.0	19.1	28.3	60.4
Assets	760.0	1,009.0	1,202.0	1,404.0	1,675.0	2,114.0	2,611.0	3,164.0	4,560.0	5,424.0
Total loans[1]	624.0	839.5	1,012.0	1,194.0	1,405.0	1,731.0	2,093.0	2,573.0	3,247.0	3,835.0
Specialized and commercial banks	584.0	748.9	884.2	1,024.0	1,206.0	1,476.0	1,759.0	2,108.0	2,638.0	3,039.0
Urban credit cooperatives	—	1.9	6.4	13.4	19.8	24.9	31.6	49.7	85.1	118.5
Rural credit cooperatives	40.0	66.9	77.1	90.9	109.5	141.1	180.9	245.4	314.4	402.4
Trust and investment companies	—	21.8	44.0	66.0	69.4	89.1	121.2	169.8	210.0	274.5
Interbank lending	40.1	55.8	70.3	72.8	84.3	105.2	134.6	169.4	667.7	800.4
Specialized and commercial banks	—	—	—	—	—	—	—	—	432.3	561.6
Urban credit cooperatives	—	1.1	2.2	3.2	5.7	7.8	10.7	17.9	61.9	57.6
Rural credit cooperatives	40.1	49.3	59.1	58.0	65.8	77.4	91.6	108.1	137.6	141.7
Trust and investment companies	—	5.4	9.0	11.6	12.8	20.0	32.3	43.4	35.9	39.5
Deposits at PBC	96.1	113.8	118.7	134.7	185.2	274.5	373.7	387.3	553.8	690.8
Specialized and commercial banks	96.1	111.6	114.0	128.9	178.2	263.8	359.3	367.8	526.7	640.7
Urban credit cooperatives	—	0.1	0.5	1.4	2.2	3.1	4.7	8.2	16.0	36.0
Rural credit cooperatives	—	—	—	—	—	—	—	—	—	—
Trust and investment companies	—	2.1	4.2	4.4	4.8	7.6	9.7	11.3	11.1	15.0
Other, net	—	—	0.9	2.3	0.9	2.9	9.4	34.7	90.7	98.5
Specialized and commercial banks	—	—	—	—	—	—	9.4	34.7	21.7	−23.1
Urban credit cooperatives	—	—	—	—	—	1.4	—	—	24.8	62.6
Rural credit cooperatives	—	—	—	2.3	0.9	1.5	—	—	44.3	59.0
Trust and investment companies	—	—	0.9	—	—	—	—	—	—	—

Source: People's Bank of China.
[1] Including portfolio of bonds.

vious year.[26] Growth in 1994 continued, albeit—owing mainly to the measures taken in 1993 to counteract the overheating of the economy—at a slower pace. The 16-Point Program, adopted in the summer of 1993, focused, among other areas, on the "leakages" in the interbank market that had been fueling inflation. Banks and NBFIs were ordered to recall before a specified date all loans "illegally" made. These were mainly loans made directly or through the interbank market to the construction and real estate and securities sectors. Loans worth about ¥ 200 billion were identified as being illegally made, of which some ¥ 40–50 billion had been made through the interbank market.

To prevent similar problems in the future, the PBC amended its guidelines on interbank activities, setting ceilings on interest rates and limits on volumes and maximum maturities of transactions according to the type of institution involved (bank or NBFI). In addition, it was also stipulated that the interbank market could no longer be used for intrabank transactions. The major effect of the new and stricter guidelines was the sharp restriction of the NBFI sector's access to the interbank market. Borrowing by trust and investment companies (TICs) had almost doubled in 1992 but decreased in actual terms in 1993 and only grew slowly in 1994. Bank borrowing and lending, however, continued growing in 1994 (see Table 2).

While China's interbank market has significantly increased its channeling of funds at the regional level, this market still looks distinctly different from a traditional interbank market for several reasons. First, participants also include NBFIs, and transactions with these institutions tend to have long maturities. Second, given the structure of the banking system, most transactions are initiated by bank branches acting in a semiautonomous way (for a long time, transactions between branches of the same bank were also conducted via the interbank market). Third, the PBC's involvement differs from center to center. Some centers only bring together bids and offers, while other centers intervene to balance the market. In fact, the PBC was reluctant for a long time to absorb any liquidity overhang in the interbank market, which is one reason why the central bank encouraged the NBFIs to become active in the market.

Primary Securities Markets

Government Securities

Treasury Bonds

After an interruption of 23 years, the Government resumed the systematic issuance of treasury bonds in 1981 through mandatory allocations to enterprises and individuals. Bonds issued between 1981 and 1984 had a maturity of ten years (Table 3). Redemption of these bonds was divided into five equal portions, with the first redemption beginning in 1986.

The role of the government securities market as an alternative to the credit plan and borrowing from the PBC is reflected in some of the methods used by the Government. In the initial years, sales of government securities were mandatory and diversified according to the holders; mandatory sales of government securities at administered rates that were negative in real terms were tantamount to taxation. Also, the administrative channels for issuing debt instruments were the same as those used to implement the credit plan. The bonds were allocated by the Ministry of Finance to the provincial governments, which, in turn, allocated them to the next administrative level and to enterprises under their jurisdiction.[27] The individuals would receive the bonds in bearer form as part of their wage payment.[28]

Over time, more market-based techniques, such as underwriting syndication, have been used (although the coupon is set administratively). The growing influence of the market is also reflected in the shortening of the maturity structure of the securities. However, the continued administered character of the government securities market is shown by the concentration of the issue period in the first half of the year, the compartmentalization of the market among issues, and the regulation of the tradability of the securities.

The predominantly retail character of the government securities market is also important. The Government has not yet really attempted to establish a wholesale market for its securities. There are several

---

[26]The difference in growth and volume between borrowing and lending in the interbank market (see also Table 2) is due to classification problems experienced by the Chinese authorities. Part of the missing funds reflect lending from state bank branches to affiliated NBFIs not reported in the PBC's statistics. In addition, some enterprises have direct access to the interbank market, a flow that is also not captured in the available statistics.

---

[27]The procedures for issuance and redemption of treasury bonds to individuals are quite complex. Each year, during the budget-planning process, the Ministry of Finance estimates the volume of securities that can be issued based on an analysis of household income and savings and, for enterprises, their financial position. Local governments bear responsibility for organizing and promoting the bond sales in their jurisdictions. The PBC's network is in charge of delivery and distribution of the bonds to the branches of the specialized banks that participate in the sales at the retail level. Actual sales of treasury bonds begin in early April of each year and can take as long as six months to complete. However, all bonds start earning interest on July 1.

[28]The treasury bonds issued to enterprises only take the form of a receipt of purchase.

Table 3. Domestic Government Debt: Total Amounts Issued by Maturity Type and Interest Rate
(In billions of yuan, unless otherwise indicated)

	1986	1987	1988	1989	1990	1991	1992	1993	1994	1995	1996	1997	1998	1999	2000	Total Volume Issued	Coupon Rate (In percent)	Inflation (Retail price index; in percent)
1981 Treasury bonds																		
To enterprises	1.0	1.0	1.0	1.0	1.0											4.8	4.0	2.4
1982 Treasury bonds																		
To enterprises		0.5	0.5	0.5	0.5	0.5										2.5	4.0	2.0
To households		0.4	0.4	0.4	0.4	0.4										2.0	8.0	
1983 Treasury bonds																		
To enterprises			0.4	0.4	0.4	0.4	0.4									2.1	4.0	1.9
To households			0.4	0.4	0.4	0.4	0.4									2.1	8.0	
1984 Treasury bonds																		
To enterprises				0.4	0.4	0.4	0.4	0.4	0.4							2.0	4.0	2.7
To households				0.4	0.4	0.4	0.4	0.4	0.4							2.2	8.0	
1985 Treasury bonds																		
To enterprises					2.2											2.2	5.0	11.9
To households					3.8											3.8	9.0	
1986 Treasury bonds																		
To enterprises						2.3										2.3	6.0	7.0
To households						4.0										4.0	10.0	
1987 Treasury bonds																		
To enterprises							2.3									2.3	6.0	8.8
To households							4.0									4.0	10.0	
1987 Other government securities																		
To enterprises					4.9											4.9	6.0	
To households					0.5											0.5	10.5	
1988 Treasury bonds																		
To enterprises						3.5										3.5	6.0	20.7
To households						5.7										5.7	10.0	
1988 Other government securities																		
To enterprises[1]					6.6											6.6	8.0	
To households					3.0											3.0	10.5	
1989 Treasury bonds																		
To households							5.6									5.6	14.0	16.3
1989 Other government securities																		
To enterprises									4.3							4.3	15.0	
To households							12.5									12.5	14.0	

1990 Treasury bonds																		1.4
To households								9.3								9.3	14.0	
1990 Other government securities																		
To enterprises										19.7[2]						19.7	15.0[3]	
To households																		
1991 Treasury bonds																		5.1
To households									19.9							19.9	9.5	
1991 Other government securities																		
To enterprises											16.0[4]					16.0	10.0	
To households																		
1992 Treasury bonds																		8.6
To households										24.6		14.8				39.4	14.0/10.5	
1992 Other government securities																		
To enterprises										9.3						9.3	10.0	
To households																		
1993 Treasury bonds																		17.0
To households											22.6		10.3			32.9	14.0/15.9	
1993 Other government securities																		
To enterprises											8.2					8.2	14.0	
To households																		
1994 Treasury bonds																		24.2
To households												70.0		1.9		71.9	15.9	
To enterprises									5.0[5]	8.3[6]						13.2	14.0/15.7	
1994 Other government securities																		
To households																		
1995 Treasury bonds																		16.3
To households												11.8[6]	20.0			31.8	12.0/14.5	
To enterprises													195.6		10.0	205.6	14.0	
Total amount maturing	1.0	1.8	2.7	3.5	24.5	18	26.0	10.1	29.2	75.2	38.6	96.6	225.9	1.9	10.0			

Sources: People's Bank of China and Ministry of Finance.
[1]Includes bonds issued to financial institutions.
[2]Includes ¥ 9.4 billion in conversion bonds.
[3]Eight percent on conversion bonds.
[4]Includes ¥ 7.0 billion conversion bonds.
[5]Six-month treasury bills issued to wholesale market.
[6]One-year treasury bills issued to wholesale market.

reasons for this policy, including the technical and administrative difficulties experienced by the Government during most of the period in managing short-term securities in paperless form. But perhaps the most important reason was the Government's targeting of the household sector to soak up purchasing power and to ensure noninflationary financing of its fiscal deficit.[29] Despite the advantages of having a retail market, too much concentration on this segment has hampered the development of a wholesale money market.

Between 1982 and 1988, the interest rate on treasury bonds issued to households was significantly higher than the interest paid on similar bonds issued to enterprises. In general, interest rates on bonds issued to individuals were set at about 1½ percentage points above the rates on savings deposits of comparable maturity. Interest payments were calculated on the basis of simple interest rates and made in full upon maturity. Administrative complications prevented the use of compounded interest rates.[30]

However, growing inflationary pressures in the mid-1980s led to resistance to mandatory allocations of government securities with negative real interest rates, particularly because some nongovernment issuers were able to offer more attractive rates. So, in order to achieve the planned sales, the Government had to shorten the maturities. The 1985 bond issue was shortened to a five-year maturity, and the maturity of the 1988 issue was further reduced to three years.

Other Government Securities

Starting in 1987, the Government began to diversify its debt instruments in response to increasing financing needs. In 1987 and 1988, the Ministry of Finance issued "key construction bonds" to households and state enterprises. Later, other debt instruments were added, such as state construction bonds and special state bonds. Most of these issues were either funds earmarked for specific projects or issues by the State Planning Commission through state investment corporations. In 1988, fiscal bonds were sold for the first time to financial institutions. The bonds, which were allocated to the banks as part of the credit plan, had a two-year maturity, and the interest rate was below the rate on bank deposits. In 1989, treasury bonds issued to enterprises were re-

named "special state bonds." Also, high inflation led the Government to issue "price-indexed bonds" in 1990, maturing in 1992.[31]

The significant shortening of maturities since the mid-1980s resulted in a "bunching" of maturities by 1990, when ¥ 24.5 billion matured (Table 3). The Government, faced with problems in repaying the full amount of maturing debt during that year, decided to roll over a total of ¥ 9.4 billion of enterprise-held bonds into five-year "conversion bonds." A similar operation took place in 1991, when ¥ 7 billion in conversion bonds were issued. A major innovation in the issuance of treasury bonds targeted for households and individuals occurred in 1991 when part of the issue was floated via an experimental underwriting syndicate and thus was no longer mandatory.[32] The Industrial and Commercial Bank of China (ICBC) group, as the lead manager, subscribed ¥ 550 million, and five comanagers each subscribed ¥ 300 million. The success of these first voluntary purchases in early 1991 led the Ministry of Finance to sell more bonds on a voluntary basis than planned during that year.

After this initial success with voluntary sales, the authorities planned to phase out mandatory sales to households over a three-year period. Voluntary sales went well in 1991 and 1992, but 1993 posed new problems. Because of very attractive returns in other markets, particularly on equities and enterprise bonds, only ¥ 4 billion out of the ¥ 33 billion offered was sold by the end of the subscription period. Even an increase in the interest rate offered did not attract sufficient investors, and, as a result, the Government returned to a policy of mandatory allocations to households.

For 1994, the Ministry of Finance planned the introduction of two new government debt instruments—treasury bills and savings bonds—besides its traditional government bonds. Two treasury bill issues took place in the first two months of the year (January 25 for the six-month bill and February 1 for the one-year bill). Both issues were underwritten by a syndicate composed of banks, NBFIs, and securities dealers on an allotment basis. The price was set by the Ministry of Finance on a fixed-rate, simple in-

---

[29]See also McKinnon (1993).

[30]Procedures are also complicated by the wide range of denominations for household-held bonds, which run from a minimum of ¥ 5 to a maximum of ¥ 100. This places heavy administrative burdens on entities involved in issuing, redeeming, and trading the bonds. In addition, all household-held bonds are issued in the same period of the year and, like all other treasury bonds, mature on July 1.

[31]The indexation mechanism ensured that the real interest rate on these bonds remained close to zero. The mechanism also applied to bank deposits with maturities of over three years. It was reintroduced in 1993, when the inflation rate again exceeded the interest rate on these financial instruments.

[32]The April 1991 underwriting was jointly organized by the Ministry of Finance, the State Commission for Restructuring the Economic System, the Stock Exchange Executive Council, and the PBC. The syndicate was composed of 58 financial institutions selected from among numerous applicants on the basis of experience in handling securities, the institution's number of counters and trading desks throughout the country, and its overall size.

terest basis at a price of 100. In both instances, the treasury bills were issued at yields higher than those on bank deposits of the same term. A major innovation was that both issues were meant mainly for the wholesale market and were placed in book-entry form through the Shanghai Securities Exchange.

The six-month treasury bill issue was well received and was oversubscribed. The one-year treasury bill, in contrast, did not sell well.[33] No other issues of these new instruments took place in 1994, and, at maturity, they were rolled over into other debt instruments. This decision reflected the Government's preference for managing debt by emphasizing the retail sector of the market (and tapping into household savings) rather than by emphasizing the banks and other financial institutions.

The other new instrument in 1994 was a savings bond tailored to retail investors. The savings bond issue had a stepped interest rate structure to encourage investors to buy and hold the bonds. The bonds also included a redemption option for investors, commencing after a holding period of six months. Issues in 1995 were also through these three types of instruments. One other experiment in 1995 concerned the issue of five-year government bonds with annual interest payments. These bonds will be more attractive to investors because of the cash flow that they provide during the bonds' life.

Nongovernment Securities

Very soon after the first issuance of government securities in 1981, the Chinese authorities allowed other market participants to issue their own debt instruments. These include enterprise shares (issued by private enterprises, as well as by state-owned enterprises (SOEs)), financial bonds issued by the specialized banks, and corporate bonds. Certificates of deposit and commercial paper emerged later, toward the turn of the decade (Chart 5).

Enterprise Shares

As early as 1982, experiments started with the issuance of enterprise shares, first for collectively owned enterprises and, in 1985, for SOEs.[34] Granting permission to collectively owned enterprises to issue shares relatively early in the reform process must be seen as a means of relieving pressure from those enterprises to compete for bank financing, as the bulk of such financing was supposed to go to the SOEs. Permitting the SOEs to issue shares was intended to reduce their reliance on bank credit.

The early issues, although called shares, differed in several important respects from the shares issued in market economies: they carried no ownership rights; they frequently offered a guaranteed minimum annual rate of return; and they often had a maturity date (between one year and five years), as well as an option of early redemption. So, in many respects, these shares were very similar to bonds. Enterprise shares owed a great deal of their attractiveness to their high returns.[35]

Corporate Bonds

Beginning in 1984, local enterprises were allowed to issue corporate bonds. Each issue had to be approved by the PBC. These bonds were allowed to pay interest up to 40 percent higher than bank deposits. Because these enterprises are state owned and state supported, treasury bonds and corporate bonds were regarded by the public to be of the same quality; hence, the large interest differential permitted for corporate bonds reduced the demand for treasury bonds and bank deposits. As the ensuing drain on bank deposits threatened the funding under the credit plan, the authorities decided in 1986 to set annual quotas under the credit plan for corporate bond issues.

Financial Bonds, Certificates of Deposit, and Commercial Paper

In 1985, banks were permitted, upon approval from the PBC, to issue financial bonds. The proceeds of these bonds were to be used to fund long-term, project-oriented bank lending. These bonds stipulated a maximum maturity (mostly of five years), but they could also be redeemed any year after the first year. The interest rate was set 2 percentage points above deposit rates of similar maturities. Since 1988, financial bonds have been marketable but, owing to the flexible redemption features, trade has remained insignificant.

While there has been increased issuing activity of certificates of deposit and commercial paper, trade in these instruments is still very limited, primarily because most people still consider them as an alternative to savings deposits and therefore hold them until maturity.

[33]The main reasons for this disappointing performance seemed to be that (i) the issue came too soon after the initial six-month issue, (ii) the maturity term offered was longer than suited investors' preferences, and (iii) the size of the offering made it difficult to place.

[34]The city of Shanghai permitted SOEs to issue shares from 1984 onward.

[35]Rates were as high as 20–40 percent in 1985–86 and even ranged between 50 percent and 100 percent in 1988 (Goldstein, Folkerts-Landau, and others (1994), p. 93).

Secondary Markets for Securities and Equity

In 1986, the Government officially authorized an experiment in secondary market trading in securities. Secondary markets developed at a fast pace shortly thereafter. At the end of the 1980s, considerable efforts were put into improving the infrastructure for secondary market trading (stock and securities exchanges and electronic networks). Despite major progress, the secondary market for government securities—still the largest component of the secondary markets—remains largely a retail market and is not completely unified. Market development is constrained by some of the features of the primary market mentioned above, such as small denominations, issue procedures, and pricing concerns. Market unification (in terms of price formation) is still not complete because of a lack of arbitrage possibilities and because of problems in delivering securities and cash when trade takes place between cities.

Initial Developments

Until 1985, securities were officially nontransferable in China. The authorities were of the view that the country lacked experience in establishing secondary markets and in correctly pricing the securities in those markets. From 1985 on, treasury bonds could be discounted at the PBC or used as collateral for loans. In addition, an unofficial secondary market gradually began operations.[36]

The first real experiment in securities trading took place in 1986 with the establishment of a secondary market for corporate bonds in Shenyang. However, trading was limited to only two bonds, and the prices were determined by the authorities. Because no fringe benefits were offered for trading such bonds, almost no transactions took place and the market remained illiquid.

In 1988, the State Council officially approved trading in government securities on an experimental basis. Trading was permitted in seven cities and only in those treasury bonds that had been sold to households in 1985–86. Two months later, trading was extended to 63 cities, and other securities were added to the list, including key construction bonds, corporate bonds, financial bonds, enterprise shares, and other nongovernment securities, such as commercial paper and certificates of deposit. Trade was also permitted in treasury bonds issued in the 1987–89 period. The 1990 issue became tradable about four months after it was floated. A few other types of securities, such as special state bonds, conversion bonds, and fiscal bonds, remained nonnegotiable.

As soon as it was legalized, securities trading gathered momentum, dominated by transactions in treasury bonds. In 1988, total trading volume in securities amounted to about ¥ 2.6 billion, of which ¥ 2.4 billion were in treasury bonds (Chart 6). This volume should be compared with the outstanding volume of the two tradable treasury bond issues of ¥ 7.9 billion. In 1989, trading volume fell slightly, mainly as a result of an official temporary freeze in the development of the securities market in the aftermath of the June 1989 events. However, total trade volume in 1990 boomed for the first time, with treasury bonds still the main security (accounting for about 88 percent of total trade, that is, ¥ 10.5 billion out of a total trade volume of ¥ 11.8 billion). The market in essence kept its retail character, as more than 80 percent of the trading was conducted on behalf of individuals. A dramatic change took place in 1992 when trade in corporate bonds for the first time exceeded trade in government securities. In 1993, while transactions in government securities and other securities stagnated, trade in corporate bonds soared even higher.

Another feature of the early years of China's secondary market was its segmented character. Insufficient communications infrastructure, the bonds' small denominations, and, most important, official restrictions on trade between cities or provinces severely restricted intercity and interregional trading. As a result, secondary market prices showed significant differences. Any attempts by dealers in cities with high demand to buy bonds in other cities at lower prices to resell in their own cities were systematically discouraged. In those early days, the Ministry of Finance took the view that government bonds should not trade below par. (On a few occasions—for example, in June 1990—both the 1987 and 1989 issues were trading below par, and the Ministry of Finance intervened in the markets to support prices through its own securities houses.)

Building the Infrastructure

Stock Exchanges

Several institutional improvements and regulatory changes were initiated in 1990–91 that gave the market a new boost and assisted in the integration of the securities markets throughout the country. First, official stock exchanges started emerging in 1990. The Government's approach toward establishing stock exchanges consisted of allowing a small number of them to open and providing investors around the country with access to those exchanges. Thus, the Shanghai Securities Exchange was officially opened

---

[36]This market was fed mainly by people who were forced to sell their securities. These securities were bought at steep discounts by speculators who redeemed them at maturity for substantial profits (Goldstein, Folkerts-Landau, and others (1994), p. 94).

Chart 6. Transactions in Debt Securities
(In billions of yuan)

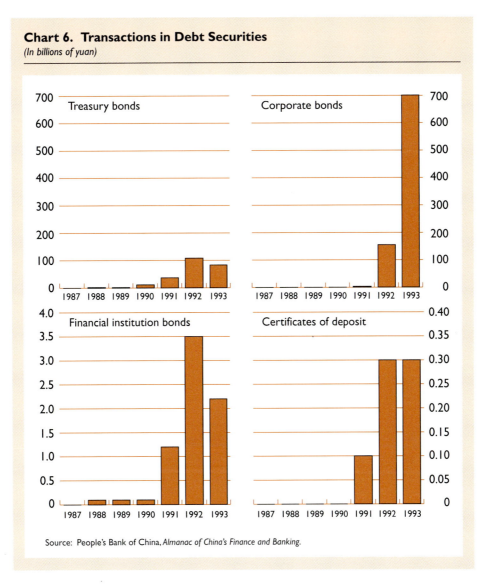

Source: People's Bank of China, *Almanac of China's Finance and Banking.*

at the end of 1990, and the Shenzhen Stock Exchange was officially recognized in the spring of 1991.[37]

[37]The establishment of these stock exchanges had been preceded by a few local experiments: in Shanghai, for example, the first official secondary market for equity was opened in 1986, starting with one trading center (organized by the Shanghai branch of the ICBC). By the end of 1988, there were 33 trading centers in the city, trading seven enterprise shares and eight bonds (Goldstein, Folkerts-Landau, and others (1994), pp. 94–95). Another experiment, not officially recognized by the central authorities, took place in Shenzhen. An over-the-counter (OTC) market emerged in 1988, mainly trading shares of the Shenzhen Development Bank. By 1990, several other shares and bonds were traded in this market, leading to a significant increase in volume that the OTC market ultimately could not handle, owing among other reasons to inefficiencies in trading practices and to a lack of appropriate regulations. The latter, in turn, led to tax evasion, insider trading, and the emergence of a curb market. In December 1990, the municipal government opened a centralized trading center that began trading in equities.

The Shanghai Securities Exchange operated under the supervision of the Shanghai PBC branch, with a representative of the PBC as one of the four members of the supervisory committee. Under the supervision of the Shanghai PBC branch, the exchange also established a centralized clearing and settlement system through an affiliated unit that provided depository services for its members. Payment and delivery are based on a book-entry system. Each member of the Shanghai Securities Exchange has to open a settlement and securities account. The member settles with the respective clearing corporation, which, in turn, has an account with its local branch of the ICBC. The Shanghai clearing corporation has established 54 settling participants and 57 government bond depositories across the country. Since the establishment of both exchanges, the number of companies with shares (A and B) listed in the exchanges has risen to

Box 4. Price Convergence in Secondary Government Securities Markets: The 1990–91 Episode

In the initial stages, when trading in government securities was first allowed, there existed almost no channels to conduct transactions between cities; even if there had been channels, such trade was highly discouraged by the local authorities. As a result, major price differences existed for the same issue of government securities, depending upon the volume of trade in a given city. Gradually, institutional developments—the establishment of stock exchanges, government securities trading centers, and electronic trading networks—have brought about a convergence in the quotations, although to date this convergence is still not complete. The government securities markets are thus not yet really integrated nationally, although trade between cities and centers has greatly increased.

The top panel of the chart presents a distribution of trade between the major cities in 1990–91, the period *par excellence* of infrastructure building in the government securities markets. On average, between 30 percent and 50 percent of total trade took place in four major cities: Shanghai, Wuhan, Guangzhou, and Shenyang. Shanghai was the most active trading city. In general, most trading activity was concentrated in the southeastern coastal cities. However, the second most important trading city was Wuhan, a more centrally located city. The share of "other cities" began growing rapidly after April 1990. The intensity of trading varied throughout the period.

The top panel also indicates that institutional improvements during the course of 1990, such as the establishment of the Quotation Center and the Securities Trading Automated Quotations System (STAQS) and the opening of the Shanghai Securities Exchange, had a significant impact on volumes traded: total trade volume increased from an average of ¥ 1.2 billion in the preceding months to ¥ 1.8 billion in December 1990. While the opening of the Shanghai Securities Exchange seems to have given a significant impetus to securities trading in general, trading in the other cities received a boost from the establishment of the electronic networks, particularly STAQS.

The bottom panel of the chart provides some indication of the role played by these institutional developments in the convergence of quotations of government securities markets. The panel presents the evolution of the differentials and average price quotation of the 1988 treasury bond issue in a sample of 36 cities with active trade in government securities in the period May 1990–April 1991. An acceleration in price convergence is observed in the period October 1990–January 1991, which coincides with the consecutive introduction of the Quotation Center, STAQS, and the Shanghai Securities Exchange.

Some additional information can be gathered from this chart. The highest prices were typically quoted in the southeast coastal area—particularly Shanghai, Hangzhou, and Nanjing—reflecting constantly high demand in this area in general and these cities in particular. Prices in the cities in that part of China were on average close to each other and close to the top end of the price spectrum (the southeast coastal region as a whole accounts for 73 percent of the highest prices). The concentration of trade in southeastern coastal cities also explains why the average prices were in general closer to the higher end.

The lowest quotations were often prices in outlying cities where markets are more supply determined. Other centers (Chongqing, for instance) show substantially varying prices, indicating that sudden supply and demand changes had a high impact on prices in markets that were still thin.

---

more than 270 (by early 1994), with combined market capitalization estimated at over ¥ 430 billion.

Electronic Networks

The rapid development of China's financial markets also set in motion the development by national and local authorities of electronic networks aimed at facilitating trading, unifying the markets by connecting several parts of the country, and enhancing the safety and security of securities trading and related payments, clearing, and settlement systems.

In September 1990, the PBC established the Quotation Center for government securities. The center provided on-line exchange of price information to securities dealers. Members communicated with the Quotation Center by telephone, providing their bid and offer prices, as well as the volumes that they intended to trade on a given date. They also communicated their trading activity of the previous day, including prices and volumes of trade. All this information was accessible by all members. However, the Quotation Center did not provide trading facilities. Given this limitation, it was quickly overtaken by other networks in 1991–92.

In 1993, the Quotation Center was transformed into the National Electronic Trading System (NETS), established by the PBC in cooperation with the state-owned specialized banks and the three national securities companies. In addition to automated trading operations, NETS also provides book-entry-based clearing and settlement facilities, mainly for shares. Thus far, virtually no bonds or government securities have been traded through NETS.

In October 1990, the Stock Exchange Executive Council, which was founded in 1989, established in

Trade Volumes and Bond Quotations in Secondary Government Securities Markets

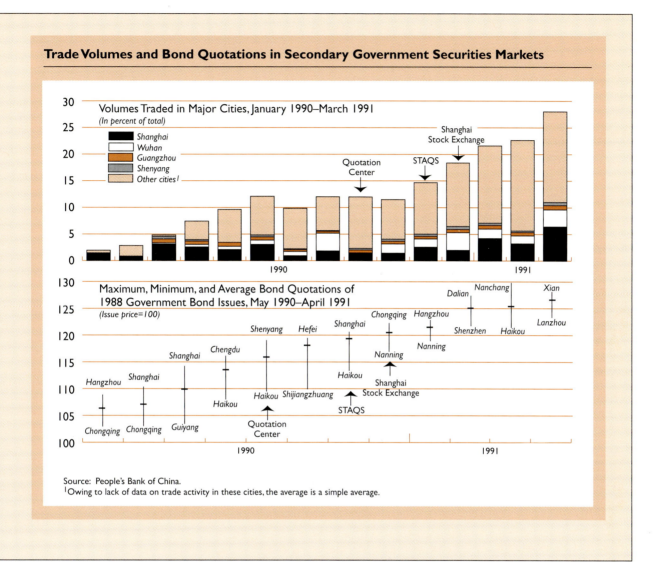

Source: People's Bank of China.
[1] Owing to lack of data on trade activity in these cities, the average is a simple average.

cooperation with the financial institutions the Securities Trading Automated Quotations System (STAQS) to promote securities market development. It is a satellite- and computer-based, over-the-counter (OTC) securities market, providing on-screen price information, as well as centralized clearing and settlement facilities. STAQS is unique in that it uses the "market maker" trading structure, under which members can be divided into two groups: those who can trade on their terminals versus those who can only receive market information. In 1995, STAQS connected 17 traders in six cities.

Other Initiatives

Secondary market development in government securities was further stimulated by other initiatives. First, government securities trading centers were es-

tablished in major cities around the country. The most active centers are Wuhan, Guangzhou, and Shenyang. Wuhan, established in 1992, is now the most active trading center in government securities. In addition to government bonds, the Wuhan exchange center also lists ten investment funds. The center has established a clearing and settlement facility, which has an account with the local PBC branch (providing next-day settlement, as indicated in Table 4). The center runs a book-entry system and provides custody services for securities. Thus far, the settlement center has established 30 branches throughout the country.

Second, several government securities were listed on the Shanghai Securities Exchange and the Shenzhen Stock Exchange. Third, the transfer of bonds from one trading center to another was legalized in October 1990, and, finally, securities

Table 4. Clearing and Settlement Procedures of Selected Exchange and Trading Systems

	Settlement Features		Delivery and Payment	Clearing Agency		Clearing agent
				Keeping of securities		
	Record date	Settlement date		Primary market	Secondary market	
Shanghai Securities Exchange	same day	next day[1]	not simultaneous[1]	exchange	exchange	ICBC
Shenzhen Stock Exchange	same day	next day	not simultaneous	exchange	local registrar	ICBC
Wuhan Securities Exchange	same day	same day	not simultaneous	exchange	exchange	PBC
NETS	next day	next day	delivery versus payment[2]	NETS	member securities firms	PBC

Sources: Shanghai Securities Exchange, Shenzhen Stock Exchange, Wuhan Securities Exchange, and NETS.

[1]A same-day settlement and delivery versus payment system was established in early 1994 for the six-month and one-year treasury bills.

[2]Delivery versus payment refers to a mechanism in an exchange-for-value settlement system that ensures that the final transfer of one asset occurs if and only if the final transfer of (an)other asset(s) occurs. Assets could include monetary assets (such as foreign exchange), securities, or other financial instruments.

trading was legalized throughout the country in March 1991. The combination of these changes, in turn, boosted the development of TICs and securities houses, as discussed in Section III. In the wake of the liberalization of trade between centers, the Shanghai Securities Exchange established links with seven securities trading centers throughout the country enabling floor members in Shanghai to buy and sell securities listed in other trading centers and vice versa. Table 4 provides an overview of the main features of the most important securities trade and exchange systems established in China in the period 1990–94. The Wuhan Securities Exchange is the only system that provides same-day settlement, while NETS is unique among the systems in that it provides delivery versus payment, which ensures that the final transfer of an asset occurs if and only if the final transfer of another asset occurs.

Legal and Regulatory Framework

The institutional changes have been supported by the introduction of a legal and regulatory framework for secondary markets. In the initial stages, local initiatives were supported by local rules and regulations. The lack of uniformity in the legal framework hindered the integration of the secondary markets at the national level. Several initiatives have been taken by the PBC since the turn of the decade to issue national legislation for securities trading and stock exchanges.

Institutional and regulatory changes not only have had a significant impact on volumes traded, but they have also stimulated price convergence. However, this convergence is not yet complete, mainly owing to a lack of arbitrage possibilities among cities and to other limitations, such as the time needed physically to transfer securities and cash from one trading center to another (see Box 4 on the previous page).

VI   Payments, Clearing, and Settlement System

Despite 16 years of economic reforms, the Chinese economy is still largely cash based. Furthermore, the share of cash payments in total payments has increased since the beginning of the reform. In the period between 1950 and the beginning of the reforms in 1978, the share of cash transactions in total financial transactions fluctuated around 5 percent, mainly because the volume of household transactions was low and payments between enterprises were effected through bookkeeping entries. Since the beginning of the 1980s, the share of cash transactions has gone up to close to 20 percent for the nation as a whole (and as high as 80 percent in some provinces), mainly owing to greater consumption activity by households, the high degree of reliance on cash by the newly emerging township and village enterprises (TVEs), and the switch to cash payments on the part of the state-owned enterprises (SOEs). The total volume of cash payments has grown tenfold since the beginning of the 1980s and now amounts to several hundred billion yuan.

Payments System

The growing reliance on cash, in combination with the growth of the economy and periods of inflation, has dramatically increased the demand for currency since the beginning of the reform. In the 1980s, the People's Bank of China (PBC) issued on average ¥ 10 billion per year. By 1994, this amount had risen to ¥ 150 billion. Currency in circulation increased from ¥ 39.6 billion in 1981 to ¥ 728.8 billion in 1994, representing an average growth of 25.1 percent per year (compared with an average GDP growth of 10.1 percent and an average inflation rate of 8.2 percent in the same period). As a result, the velocity of currency in circulation declined from 12 in 1981 to 6 in 1994. During the same period, the share of currency in M1 increased from 24.2 percent to 35.4 percent.

Even though the latter percentage is not excessively high according to international standards, changes in the level of currency in circulation are

important because of their political sensitivity: cash is still seen as the engine of the economy. This political attention is also the main reason that the cash plan still plays an important part in the formulation of the country's financial policies. However, the cash plan, which used to be mandatory, has lately been treated as more indicative than prescriptive (Box 5).

The increasing reliance on cash since the start of the reforms—and, more particularly, since the beginning of the 1990s—has put the demand for currency and the cash plan even more in the spotlight than before. The PBC's ability to control liquidity in the economy is hampered because the cash part of money demand is controlled by the State Council and subject to a host of political influences. This situation tends to generate friction between the PBC and other government agencies as their respective objectives are often at odds. The increasing reliance on cash in China mainly stems from a combination of factors, such as the lack of generally accessible alternative payments instruments in the economy, the lack of confidence in those alternative payments instruments that do exist (until 1995, there was no legal framework underpinning the use of negotiable payments instruments), the lack of confidence of the banking system in the collective enterprise sector, and the inefficiencies and imperfections of the payments, clearing, and settlement system.

A considerable part of bank credit, notably but not only to the agricultural sector, is still in the form of cash. The transactions of the TVE sector—a sector that is now larger than the SOE sector in terms of output—are still mainly cash based because of the difficulties that those enterprises experience in getting access to the traditional banking sector. The buildup in recent years of interenterprise arrears among SOEs is another reason for this sector's increasing reliance on cash. Wages are generally paid in cash. Experiments in selected cities and sectors have been undertaken to pay wages in savings deposits, but, owing to the lack of such alternative payments instruments as checks, workers almost immediately withdraw the funds from their accounts. In general, only a small portion of households have

---

Box 5. The Cash Plan

The cash plan is prepared by the People's Bank of China (PBC) at the end of each year, based on estimates received from the municipal and prefecture level. The expected demand for currency is calculated using (i) the real growth rate of the economy, (ii) expectations with respect to inflation, (iii) the growth of fixed-asset investment, (iv) the growth of the consumption fund,[1] and (v) requirements for agricultural production. This bottom-up procedure in itself introduces an expansionary bias into the plan.

Final approval of the cash plan is in the hands of the State Council, following input from different ministries and the State Planning Commission, a process that tends to increase the expansionary bias. The cash plan is broken down by provinces, based on the growth rate of industry and agriculture in each province, the planned volume of investments per province, and the regional inflation rates. The PBC is in charge of implementing the plan during the year. The cash plan is usually revised in the middle of the year, based on recent economic developments and forecasts. The PBC has almost no control over the factors affecting currency in circulation, and its role is essentially to monitor cash flows and alert the authorities when deviations from the cash plan have occurred.

---

[1]This item relates to wages, salaries, and pensions payable by enterprises and state administrative units, plus an estimate of other administrative expenses.

---

current accounts and the use of checks is very limited. (For a long time, individuals could not hold checking accounts with banks for administrative reasons.)

At the end of 1993, vault cash of enterprises amounted to ¥ 132.4 billion, or 22.6 percent of total currency in circulation. The farming sector held another 46.5 percent, urban households 20.1 percent, and the remaining 10.8 percent was in the hands of the so-called floating population (People's Bank of China (1994a)).

Efforts have been undertaken in some provinces to stimulate both the development of new payments instruments and confidence in their use. For instance, the introduction since 1989 of promissory notes, checks, and commercial paper in Jiangsu Province reduced the proportion of cash payments from 7 percent in 1990 to 3.3 percent in 1994. Debit cards have been sold by banks since 1989 in selected cities.[38] Recently, banks in some cities have also

---

[38]In the first year, about 200,000 debit cards were issued, with an annual turnover of ¥ 3.3 billion (World Bank (1990)).

---

started selling credit cards. Thus far, such experiments have remained the exception rather than the rule. On the contrary, the share of cash payments in total payments is still increasing in many parts of the country. In some southern provinces, the practice of placing a premium on the use of cash has been gaining importance. In addition, the growth in interenterprise arrears and increased drug trafficking, as well as smuggling and tax evasion, are further stimulating the use of cash.

Clearing and Settlement System

China's payments, clearing, and settlement system was established in the 1950s, partly based on the Soviet model. Noncash payments are mainly done through checks, mail transfers, and bank drafts. Intracity, business-related payments are done by check or credit transfers and cleared locally. Out-of-town payments are conducted through mail transfers, bank drafts, or telegraphic transfers, as checks are not accepted outside the town or city clearing region. Other instruments used in business-related payments include promissory notes, bank drafts, and trade bills of exchange. Reflecting the administrative structure of the banking system, each bank branch within the same clearing zone clears both intrabank and interbank as if it were an autonomous bank, because each branch has a clearing account with the local PBC branch.

The rapid development of China's financial system since the middle of the 1980s put considerably more pressure on the operational capacity of the existing payments system. In 1986, in an effort to cope with these problems, the PBC undertook many initiatives to improve the payments system, including the development of an electronic payments system; the expansion of the number and geographic coverage of local clearinghouses; the use of microcomputers; the introduction of automated check-processing equipment; and the initiation of some standardization and coding systems.

While all these improvements were significant, the most important one was the development of an electronic payments system, the satellite-based Electronic Interbank System (EIS), by a wholly owned PBC subsidiary. The EIS became operational in November 1991. It is managed under the leadership of the PBC and was designed as a system for large-value transfers (payments exceeding ¥ 100,000) between the PBC branches on a gross basis. The system is primarily designed to deal with credit transfers (payment orders) but can also handle a small number of debit payments. The EIS links PBC branches in 416 cities using the X.25 Protocol. Of those 416 cities, 300 are actively using the system for large-value transfers.[39] Connected PBC branches also use the system to transmit statistical, accounting, and banking supervision data to PBC headquarters in Beijing. While transactions are reported to move rapidly point to point (in seven seconds), settlement is on a next-day basis. Perhaps this lag is attributable to the need for manual intervention to net total daily activity and post entries to the 3,500 connected PBC branch accounts. Even though the EIS marked a major improvement over the previous system, it is still not equipped to deal with the large-value payments common to an active money market. This is also one of the main reasons for the delay in the development of nationally integrated money and capital markets.

In the late 1980s, work started on a completely new payments and clearing system, China's National Automated Payments System. The new system is planned to be implemented throughout the entire country by the year 2000 (pilot projects in parts of the country will start as early as 1997). The system will rely on a common information carrier based on the X.25 Protocol, which will link all PBC branches (2,500 at present) throughout the country and provide direct access to financial institutions. The carrier will provide communications services between specialized bank branches via the local PBC branches, with a capacity to carry approximately 50 million payment transactions per day. The system will comprise a bulk electronic system for retail payments (featuring multilateral net settlement), a large-value transfer system (the settlement system of which has yet to be determined), and a book-entry system (at this stage, available for government securities only).

---

[39]Financial institutions have no direct access to the system. Their interbank transactions are serviced by and through PBC branches. In general, each branch of each financial institution has two accounts at the PBC branch at the same administrative level: a required reserve account and an excess reserve account. The latter is used for payments and settlement purposes.

VII   Instruments of Monetary Policy and Monetary Developments

Prior to the reforms, monetary policy was implemented through the credit plan and the cash plan. As the credit plan was the financial counterpart of the physical or investment plan, it specified the amount of credit needed by enterprises to implement their output targets. Monetary policy was thus a passive instrument in the execution of the Government's objectives. As described in the preceding section, the cash plan covered the various factors that influenced the amount of cash in the economy and, as such, complemented the credit plan.

The Operating Framework

Reflecting the coexistence since 1979 in the economy of planning devices and market mechanisms, the operating procedures for monetary policy underwent gradual changes. In the process, monetary policy acquired a more independent role as a tool for macroeconomic management. In this new environment, however, the operating procedures had to meet several requirements that were often contradictory.

First, the priorities of the Government had to be met through the credit plan while the emerging non-state-owned industrial sector had to be given access to bank financing. Second, to be effective as a macroeconomic tool, the operating procedures of monetary policy had to remain in line with the changing institutional structure of the financial system and the gradually increasing openness of China's economy. Third, in this changing environment, the People's Bank of China (PBC) had to pursue two objectives that were often conflicting: the credit plan, with its inherent expansionary and inflationary bias, remained the primary objective of the Government's policy, but at the same time the PBC was supposed to use monetary policy actions to control inflation.

The potential for conflicts can perhaps be best conveyed by the fact that, in its transformation to a genuine central bank, the PBC's mandate was never explicitly changed from de facto lender of *first* resort in the command economy to that of lender of *last* resort in a market environment. The dilemma posed by these two objectives was never really addressed in the period before 1992–93 (when work on a new law started) and was at the origin of shortcomings in the PBC's ability in responding to monetary developments.

The operating procedures for monetary policy evolved into a dual-control system as indirect control methods gradually supplemented direct controls; however, the dilemmas inherent in such a dual-control system were also present. The credit plan remained the core policy instrument, but its formulation underwent changes as macroeconomic considerations were increasingly taken into account. In addition, the credit plan's implementation was at times relaxed as banks were given more freedom to set their lending rates. Particularly since the second half of the 1980s, however, the credit quotas (derived from the plan) lost part of their effectiveness because of changes in the financial sector.[40]

Indirect instruments—reserve requirements, PBC lending to banks, and more frequent interest rate changes—were introduced as soon as the PBC started operating in 1984–85. These instruments were meant to supplement the credit quotas to enable the PBC to respond more flexibly to changing conditions. "Window guidance," or moral suasion, has also been used to some extent as an instrument of monetary policy.

However, the continuing demands placed on the financial system by policy loans constrained the flexibility and effectiveness of these alternative control methods throughout most of the period. These limitations are clearly seen in the role played by interest rates. They were used increasingly to control monetary aggregates, but their effectiveness remained limited, in part because the "soft" budget constraints of state-owned enterprises (SOEs) made those enterprises unresponsive to the cost of borrowing. In fact, the impact of interest rate changes was felt much more on household savings than on bank lending.

---

[40]The PBC uses the term "credit quota" instead of credit ceilings.

Moreover, the so-called indirect methods were not necessarily used to influence the markets (as they are intended to) but as substitutes for money markets. Since the mid-1980s, two instruments—PBC lending to specialized banks and reserve requirements—have been used throughout the country to adjust shortages or excesses of liquidity that would otherwise be leveled out by an integrated interbank market.

The decision in 1993 of the Third Plenum to move to a market economy included the adoption of indirect instruments to guide macroeconomic development. As a result, the PBC started preparations in 1993 for the introduction of open market operations as its main monetary policy instrument, with reserve requirements and PBC lending to banks as its supporting instruments. The credit plan was to be phased out gradually by replacing it with asset-liability management ratios to manage assets and liabilities and an increasing reliance on indirect instruments until such time as this reliance could be total. As part of the transition, direct PBC credit to the Government was discontinued in early 1994—more than a year before the new PBC law enshrined this decision—and the authorities contemplated using the interest rate instrument more actively (by changing the administratively set rates more frequently).

The reforms in the foreign exchange system of early 1994 had important consequences for monetary management. The liberalization of foreign exchange transactions is a potential source of inflows and outflows of liquidity, given the authorities' objective to stabilize the exchange rate. Thus, these reforms have increased the need for active liquidity management based on the use of indirect monetary policy instruments.

Because it takes time to develop the appropriate infrastructure to conduct indirect monetary policy effectively, the PBC, in its fight against inflation, has been forced to rely on several ad hoc instruments since 1992. As will be discussed in a subsequent subsection, the PBC issued finance bills (a type of central bank bill) in 1993, and the PBC attracted excess liquidity by offering special deposits at the central bank in 1994 and 1995.

The Credit Plan

In the past, the credit plan served simply as the financial counterpart to the Government's investment plan. As a result, it was formulated as a "bottom-up" exercise focusing on the credit needs of borrowers for planned output targets (see Box 6). The first change took place in the early 1980s when banks were given more discretion to lend working capital, thereby allowing them to depart somewhat from the credit quotas. This change concerned only the process of implementing—not formulating—the credit plan.

Second, changing economic conditions in the mid-1980s influenced the monitoring and implementation of the credit plan and the related quota framework. In the period 1986–88, credit quotas became merely indicative targets, and overshooting was not penalized. On other occasions, particularly during the 1989 austerity period, the quotas were more strictly enforced, and the proportion of directed credit increased.

Third, in line with the diversification of the financial system, the scope of the credit plan was broadened in 1988 to include credit to nonbank financial institutions (NBFIs) and direct financing of enterprises, in addition to credit to specialized and universal banks. However, the narrow credit plan, which set credit quotas for specialized and universal banks, remained the core plan; it was monitored more closely by the PBC and was the only plan that needed approval by the State Council.[41]

Finally, a significant departure from the traditional formulation took place in the latter part of the 1980s when the PBC began to evaluate the consistency of the credit plan with the broader macroeconomic objectives of price stability, the balance of payments, and economic growth. The target for aggregate domestic credit was formulated in line with money supply targets and no longer as a purely bottom-up process; it thus signaled the authorities' recognition of the increasing role of market mechanisms in China's economy.

However, this change in procedures also brought to the surface the potential conflicts involved in implementing such a plan in an economy that is adopting market mechanisms. The credit plan is a compromise among three agencies: the State Planning Commission (whose interest lies in assuring that the plan provides sufficient funds for investments under the five-year plans); the Ministry of Finance (which tries to minimize the budgetary costs of financing loss-making SOEs and, therefore, aims to include as much as possible of this funding in the credit plan); and the PBC (which tries to ensure macroeconomic stability).

The above changes follow from a combination of, on the one hand, the PBC's willingness to downplay the role of the credit plan as a monetary policy tool in a changing environment and, on the other hand, the reluctance of the political authorities to give up the credit plan, as well as the PBC's inability to rely on other instruments when monetary policy needs to be tightened.

The accelerated move since 1992 toward indirect instruments of monetary policy led the PBC to de-

---

[41]The specialized and universal banks are responsible for over 80 percent of the total credit in the economy (see Chart 4).

Box 6. The Credit Plan

Prior to the economic reforms in China, the credit plan, together with the cash plan (see Box 5), the central government budget, and the foreign exchange plan, represented the (subordinate) financing side of the physical plan. Even though the emphasis has shifted during the reform years, these plans must still be drafted.

Several basic principles underlie the credit plan. Some of the methods and principles have undergone modifications during the reform period. The credit plan is developed annually by three agencies—the People's Bank of China (PBC), the Ministry of Finance, and the State Planning Commission—and is subject to approval by the State Council. The need for credit at the macroeconomic level is determined by the State Council's targets for output growth, investment, and inflation. At the microeconomic level, a bottom-up aggregation of sectoral and local funding needs is passed on by the local authorities to the provincial authorities and finally to the national authorities. Whereas the credit plan during most of the 1980s was basically a bottom-up process with an inherent expansionary bias, the PBC has tried since the end of the 1980s to make the plan consistent with macroeconomic targets, such as real growth and inflation.

The credit plan is implemented through a set of credit quotas for each specialized and universal bank. In addition, ceilings are set on access to PBC lending for the banks and on direct financing of enterprises (through enterprise bonds and shares). The PBC headquarters also sets aside a portion of the aggregate credit ceiling for PBC branches to use at their own discretion in their regions.

The PBC allocates annual credit quotas to the head office of each specialized and universal bank, which, in turn, allocates quotas to its subordinate branches. The credit plan also sets subceilings for specific types of loans, and, since 1990, nonbinding quarterly credit ceilings—in addition to the annual ceilings—have been in place. The PBC headquarters also allocates separate credit quotas for the PBC branches in Shanghai and Shenzhen, which, in turn, allocate quotas to the specialized and universal banks in their respective regions. The PBC thus derives quotas for credit by region, as well as by bank branch, in order to control credit aggregates.

The allocation of credit quotas among specialized and universal banks is based on each bank's loan share during the previous year, as well as on the importance of the sectoral credit that the bank provides under the overall investment plan. The monitoring of credit quotas of individual bank branches is done both vertically, by the headquarters of specialized and universal banks, and horizontally, by the local branches of the PBC, which control credit quotas within their regions. PBC branches, in turn, make quarterly reports to the PBC headquarters, which adjusts credit quotas among regions as required by changing credit needs.

Starting in 1988, the authorities made a distinction between the central credit plan as described above and the broader credit plan. The latter includes lending by rural credit cooperatives (RCCs) and all other nonbank financial institutions (NBFIs), with the exception of financial leasing companies. The broader credit plan has a more indicative character than the central credit plan. The PBC headquarters, in consultation with its branches and the Agricultural Bank of China, determines ceilings for the overall credit expansion of RCCs, while other NBFIs are governed by the PBC alone. The PBC assigns credit quotas to the local PBC branches for the NBFIs in their regions. These quotas apply only to the total credit of NBFIs and are monitored on an annual basis. Direct financing of enterprises, in the form of enterprise bonds, has also been subject to credit quotas. By bringing credit to NBFIs and direct financing of enterprises under the credit plan, the PBC hoped to be better able to manage and control the aggregate credit needs of the economy.

As part of the reforms contemplated in the wake of the 1993 decision to expedite financial sector reform, the authorities have adopted a plan to gradually phase out the credit plan. The 1995 credit plan applied only to the four state commercial banks and the four universal banks (the Bank of Communications, the China International Trust and Investment Corporation's Industrial Bank, Hua Xia Bank, and China Everbright Bank). The lending activities of all other banks and NBFIs are to be guided by the loan-to-deposit ratio. As soon as the eight aforementioned banks are deemed ready to comply with the loan-to-deposit ratio and other specified ratios, the credit plan will be phased out altogether.

---

velop a strategy for phasing out the credit plan after 1994. In 1995, only the four state commercial banks and the four universal (or nationwide commercial) banks were subject to formal credit quotas. All other banks' lending activities were guided by the loan-to-deposit ratio. The phasing out of credit quotas for the state commercial banks is planned to take place within the next two years, but this action will depend on these banks' ability to match loans and deposits (and thus reduce their reliance on borrowing from the PBC).

PBC Lending Facilities

In 1984, PBC lending to specialized banks was introduced to manage overall bank liquidity and to enable banks to meet their credit plan targets by filling the resource gap between bank deposits and lending. PBC lending comprises four different types of lending:

- *Annual lending*, which carries maturities of one to two years, is primarily the directed credit required to meet planned output targets;

- *Seasonal lending*, with maturities of two to four months, mainly covers the seasonal withdrawal of deposits;
- *Daily lending* carries maturities of up to ten days; and
- A *rediscount facility*, mainly for commercial paper, has maturities of six months to provide additional resources to specialized banks during the year.

At the end of the 1980s, an average of 60 percent of total PBC lending to specialized banks was annual lending, with seasonal and daily lending accounting for 35 percent and 5 percent of the total, respectively. With annual lending as the dominant component, the PBC lending facility was thus closely linked to the credit plan.

In principle, PBC credit is extended to specialized banks only, but a number of NBFIs have been approved by the PBC to access its credit facilities.[42] In order to borrow under their annual and quarterly quotas from the PBC, specialized banks and approved NBFIs are required to submit applications to PBC headquarters stating the loan amount and maturity, as well as the intended use of borrowed funds and the capacity to repay.[43] In the first years of the PBC lending facilities, PBC branches had significant autonomy in providing credit to financial institutions in their jurisdictions on the basis of "own resources," which consisted of excess reserves and loan recoveries from financial institutions, as well as of deposits of government bodies and the post office. In this way, PBC branches were encouraged to increase their loan recoveries and mobilization of funds. Pressure from regional and local governments, however, contributed to an increase in lending by the branches of the PBC, which, in turn, contributed to inflationary pressures.

As a result, the PBC increased its control over credit creation in 1989 as part of the austerity program by requiring its branches to transfer to a headquarters account all deposits from financial institutions (including excess reserves), as well as deposits of government bodies and the post office. So, while PBC branches still had some funds to use at their own discretion, their lending capacity was limited to

resources that they received from headquarters. The Shanghai and Shenzhen branches retained their autonomy in decisions on lending to financial institutions in their respective regions.

In recent years, PBC lending facilities were further reformed to dissociate the instrument from the credit plan and to transform it into an instrument for liquidity management. As part of the 16-Point Program, the PBC started calling back loans to state-owned specialized banks and other financial institutions as a mechanism to control liquidity. In 1994, the decision was taken to centralize most PBC lending at the headquarters level, thereby forcing the banks to improve their internal liquidity management. The rediscount window is still operated at the branch level under a ceiling allocated by the PBC headquarters.

Reserve Requirements

Reserve requirements were introduced in 1984 to influence liquidity and liquidity distribution in the financial system. For the first year, the redeposit rates were differentiated according to the type of deposit: 40 percent on urban household deposits, 20 percent on enterprise deposits, and 25 percent on rural deposits (De Wulf and Goldsbrough (1986), p. 228). In 1985, the requirement was reduced and made uniform at 10 percent for all domestic currency deposits of specialized and universal banks, rural credit cooperatives (RCCs), urban credit cooperatives (UCCs), and trust and investment companies (TICs).[44] In response to the need to tighten monetary policy, the ratio was increased to 12 percent in 1987 and to 13 percent in 1988.

In an effort to tighten its monetary policy stance further, the PBC supplemented the required reserves in 1989 by effecting guidelines on "excess reserve requirements" in the range of 5–7 percent of domestic currency deposits. The rationale for introducing these guidelines was partly to sterilize the lending capacity of specialized banks, given the high level of excess reserves at the time, but also to serve as a cushion in light of the shallowness of the interbank market and the inefficiencies of the payments, clearing, and settlement system.

---

[42]Approval of NBFIs to borrow from the PBC is based on both balance sheet and profitability considerations. Approved NBFIs that wish to borrow from the PBC are required to open settlement accounts with the PBC. NBFIs can only borrow from the PBC twice a year.

[43]Annual quotas are based on the market share of financial institutions, as well as on the extent to which they engage in policy lending. The PBC can adjust its lending quota for a specific bank or adjust the allocation of its lending among banks, as necessary, during the year, taking into account the growth of deposits relative to credit ceilings of specialized banks, as well as the overall liquidity situation of the financial sector and the changing needs of priority sectors of the economy.

---

[44]Since then, reserve requirements have been refined to cover demand and savings deposits of specialized banks and to exclude fiscal deposits. Interbank deposits are also excluded from reserve requirements. Trust deposits of other financial institutions with specialized banks are subject to reserve requirements.

Required reserves of RCCs are deposited with the Agricultural Bank of China (ABC). These deposits with the ABC are, in turn, subject to reserve requirements. UCCs deposit their required reserves directly with the PBC. The reserve ratio for UCCs, however, differs somewhat from other banking institutions; it is in the range of 10–20 percent of deposits, at the discretion of individual cooperatives.

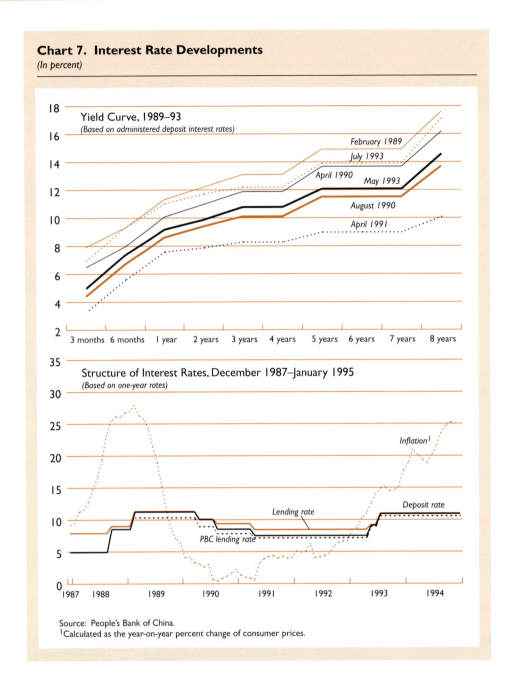

Chart 7. Interest Rate Developments
(In percent)

Yield Curve, 1989–93
(Based on administered deposit interest rates)

February 1989
July 1993
April 1990
May 1993
August 1990
April 1991

3 months 6 months 1 year 2 years 3 years 4 years 5 years 6 years 7 years 8 years

Structure of Interest Rates, December 1987–January 1995
(Based on one-year rates)

Inflation[1]

Lending rate
Deposit rate
PBC lending rate

1987   1988   1989   1990   1991   1992   1993   1994

Source: People's Bank of China.
[1]Calculated as the year-on-year percent change of consumer prices.

To meet the requirements, banks are required to keep reserve accounts at the PBC. Required and excess reserves are remunerated at the same interest rate. Compliance is based on outstanding deposits at the end of each month. In practice, however, banks adjust the accounts every ten days. Shortfalls in the required reserves are subject to a penalty interest rate of 4 basis points of the shortage a day. The excess reserve requirement can be seen as a second tier of reserves that has to be held on an average basis, as banks can use these reserves for settlements of payments, interbank lending, or cash withdrawals.

So, technically speaking, the two-tier reserve requirement system amounts de facto to one single requirement of 18–20 percent of banks' deposits, to be met on an average basis. In fact, there can never be a shortfall in the legal reserve requirement because of the cushion provided by the excess reserve requirement.

Mainly because of the administrative organization of the PBC and the specialized banks, required and excess reserves are held by each branch of each bank at the PBC branch at the same administrative level. Consequently, monitoring is also done at the

Table 5. Selected Interest Rates on Loans
(In percent)

	1987	1988 Sept.	1989 Feb.	1990 Apr.	1990 Aug.	1991 Apr.	1991 Oct.	1993 May	1993 July	1995 Jan.
State industrial and commercial loans										
Working capital	7.92	9.00	11.34	10.08	9.36	8.64	8.64	9.36	10.98	10.98
Fixed-asset loans										
One year	7.92	9.00	11.34	10.08	9.36	8.46	8.46	9.18	10.98	11.70
One–three years	8.64	9.90	12.78	10.80	10.08	9.00	9.00	10.80	12.24	12.96
Three–five years	9.36	10.80	14.40	11.52	10.80	9.54	9.54	12.06	13.86	14.58
Five–ten years	10.08	13.32	19.26	11.88	11.16	9.72	9.72	12.24	14.04	14.76
Over ten years	10.80	16.20	24.00	11.88	11.16	9.72	9.72	12.24	14.04	14.76
Agricultural loans										
Crop production	7.92	9.00	10.08	9.00	8.28	7.74	7.74	8.46	10.08	10.08
Crop investment										
One year	5.76	9.00	11.34	10.08	9.36	8.64	8.64	9.18	10.98	11.70
One-three years	6.48	9.90	12.78	10.80	9.36	8.64	8.64	10.80	12.24	12.96
Three-five years	7.20	10.80	14.40	11.52	10.08	9.54	9.54	12.06	13.86	14.58
Over five years	7.92	13.32	19.26	11.88	10.08	9.54	9.54	12.24	14.04	14.76
Household loans										
Agriculture	7.92	9.00	11.34	10.08	9.36	8.64	8.64	9.36	10.98	10.98
Industry and commerce	9.36–11.00	11.70	14.74	12.10	11.23	10.37	10.37	11.23	13.18	13.18
Working capital for township enteprises	8.64	9.00	11.34	10.80	9.36	8.64	8.64	9.36	10.98	10.98

Source: People's Bank of China.

branch level. This arrangement has several implications. Monitoring by the PBC of required and excess (or free) reserves on a systemwide basis is complicated and time-consuming, and thus takes place with considerable delays. In addition, to adjust their reserve positions with the PBC, bank branches have to go to the interbank market because smoothly working intrabank communications are lacking.

A first measure to link reserve requirements better to liquidity monitoring and management was the decision taken in 1995 to have banks meet their excess reserve guidelines on a consolidated (bankwide) basis. In a system in which bank branches mostly operate autonomously, this measure was a significant step in the direction of centralized liquidity management. This change gives the commercial banks more responsibility in internally managing their reserves, while giving the PBC a better overview of liquidity developments in the system and improving its ability to assess those developments and to decide on the amount and timing of the market interventions needed to mop up or inject liquidity.

Interest Rates

Because the financial system has been seen as a discretionary allocative tool, China's interest rate structure has always been very complex, with more than 50 rates administered by the PBC.[45] On the lending side, besides the basic distinction made between working capital loans (of different maturities) and fixed-assets loans, industrial and commercial loans, agricultural loans, and household loans are treated differently. On the deposit side, a distinction is made between individual and institutional depositors, and the PBC sets rates for sight deposits, three- and six-month deposits, and deposits of one, two, three, five, and eight years.

Starting in 1985, and particularly since 1988, interest rates have been adjusted more frequently, primarily in response to inflationary pressures, but also because of the profitability considerations of enterprises and specialized banks (Chart 7 and Tables 5 and 6). Banks were also allowed to adjust loan rates within a 10 percent margin above the administered rate.[46] There was no such flexibility, however, for deposit rates.[47] The austerity program of 1989 reversed this partial interest rate liberaliza-

[45]Interest rates are administered by the PBC, but changes in the rates need prior approval by the State Council.
[46]That is, if the administered rate is 10 percent, banks can charge between 10 percent and 11 percent.
[47]Only UCCs and RCCs were allowed some flexibility in setting deposit rates within prespecified margins.

Table 6. Interest on Deposits, PBC Operations, and Interbank Market
(In percent)

	1987	1988 Sept.	1989 Feb.	1990 Apr.	1990 Aug.	1991 Apr.	1991 Oct.	1993 May	1993 July	1995 Jan.
Individual deposits										
Sight	2.88	2.88	2.88	2.88	2.16	1.80	1.80	2.16	3.15	3.15
Three months	...	...	7.56	6.30	4.32	3.24	3.24	4.86	6.66	6.66
Six months	6.12	6.48	9.00	7.74	6.48	5.40	5.40	7.20	9.00	9.00
One year	7.20	8.64	11.34	10.08	8.64	7.56	7.56	9.18	10.98	10.98
Two years	...	9.18	12.24	10.98	9.36	7.92	7.92	9.90	11.70	11.70
Three years	8.28	9.72	13.14	11.88	10.08	8.28	8.28	10.80	12.24	12.24
Five years	9.36	10.80	14.94	13.68	11.52	9.00	9.00	12.06	13.86	13.86
Eight years	10.44	12.42	17.64	16.20	13.68	10.08	10.08	14.58	17.10	17.10
Institutional deposits										
Sight	1.80	2.88	2.88	2.88	2.16	1.80	1.80	2.16	3.15	3.15
Three months	...	...	7.56	6.30	4.32	3.24	3.24	4.86	6.66	6.66
Six months	4.32	6.48	9.00	7.74	6.48	5.40	5.40	7.20	9.00	9.00
One year	5.04	8.64	11.34	10.08	8.64	7.56	7.56	9.18	10.98	10.98
Two years	5.76	9.18	12.24	10.98	9.36	7.92	7.92	9.90	11.70	11.70
Three years	6.48	9.72	13.14	11.88	10.08	8.28	8.28	10.80	12.24	12.24
Five years	...	10.80	14.94	13.68	11.52	9.00	9.00	12.06	13.86	13.86
Eight years	...	12.42	17.64	16.20	13.68	10.08	10.08	14.58	17.10	17.10
PBC rates										
Loans to financial institutions										
One year (planned)	7.20	8.28	10.44	9.00	7.92	7.20	7.20	9.00	10.62	10.89
Seasonal	7.20	7.56	9.72	9.00	7.92	7.20	7.20			
6 months or less								8.82	10.44	10.71
3 months or less								8.64	10.26	10.44
7–20 days	6.48	8.28	9.00	9.00	7.92	7.20	7.20	8.46	10.08	10.32
Interest on reserves										
Required reserves	4.32	5.04	7.20	7.92	6.84	6.12	6.12	7.56	9.18	9.18
Excess reserves	5.76	6.48	8.60	7.92	6.84	6.12	6.12	7.56	9.18	9.18
Interbank market rate[1]	Free	Free	Free							

Source: People's Bank of China.
[1]Regulated by the PBC from April 1990 to July 1993. From January 1995, not more than 13.176 percent (20 percent above working capital loans).

tion, which was not resumed until the early 1990s when the austerity period had ended and banks were again allowed to set their lending rates within prespecified margins. This margin has been 60 percent for RCCs, 30 percent for UCCs, and 20 percent for the other banking institutions.[48] Until the reform of the interbank market in early 1996, interest rate regulations applied also to interbank transactions. The ceiling on the interbank rate was equal to the interest rate on working capital loans plus 20 percent.

The introduction of more flexibility in interest rates seems to have been constrained by at least

three factors. First, the need for prior State Council approval for each rate change made the process cumbersome and lengthy. Second, during most of the period, the authorities' interest rate policy was directed toward two often-conflicting goals: to encourage long-term savings mobilization and to facilitate borrowing by SOEs—particularly those with financial problems. Pursuing these objectives often led to inconsistencies, such as higher interest rates for deposits than loans over the same period, which resulted in negative interest rate margins for banks (Table 7). In general, the margins between most lending and deposit rates of equivalent duration remained very narrow. To resolve these inconsistencies, the authorities resorted to using an indexation scheme for long-term deposit rates in times of high inflation. This scheme allowed them to keep lending rates low while maintaining attractive deposit rates.

---

[48]In practice, in northeastern and northwestern China, where there are more loss-making SOEs, banks charge the official rates; in the coastal areas, banks usually lend at rates close to the ceiling of the range or even at rates above the permitted floating range.

Table 7. Margins on Selected Maturities
(In percent)

	1987	1988 Sept.	1989 Feb.	1990 Apr.	1990 Aug.	1991 Apr.	1991 Oct.	1993 May	1993 July	1995 Jan.
Fixed-asset loans										
One year	7.90	9.00	11.34	10.08	9.36	8.46	8.46	9.18	10.98	11.70
Five years	10.10	13.30	19.26	11.88	11.16	9.72	9.72	12.24	14.04	14.76
Five–ten years	10.10	13.30	19.26	11.88	11.16	9.72	9.72	12.24	14.04	14.76
Deposits from individuals										
One year	7.20	8.60	11.34	10.08	8.64	7.56	7.56	9.18	10.98	10.98
Five years	9.40	10.80	14.94	13.68	11.52	9.00	9.00	12.06	13.86	13.86
Eight years	10.40	12.40	17.64	16.20	13.68	10.08	10.08	14.58	17.10	17.10
Margins										
One year	0.72	0.36	—	—	0.72	0.90	0.90	—	—	0.72
Five years	0.72	2.52	4.32	−1.80	−0.36	0.72	0.72	0.18	0.18	0.90
Above ten years	−0.36	0.90	1.62	−4.32	−2.52	−0.36	−0.36	−2.34	−3.06	−2.34

Source: People's Bank of China.

The scheme was used for the first time in 1988, when inflation started building up.[49] Third, the heavy reliance by the specialized banks on borrowing from the PBC—up to one third of their resources—proved to be another constraining factor, as changes in the PBC's lending rates affected the average cost of the banks' resources directly and dramatically.

Open Market Operations

The PBC began using open-market-type operations in 1993 to influence the level of liquidity in the financial system.[50] In that year, the central bank issued central bank bills in the amount of ¥ 20 billion to absorb excess liquidity in some parts of the country (and to redistribute it to areas with shortages). In 1994 and 1995, the PBC offered the banks special deposits at attractive interest rates to further absorb the excess liquidity in the system.[51] These instruments

[49]Since then, the indexation mechanism has gone into effect every time that the inflation rate exceeds the three-year deposit rate. The mechanism broadly ensures that the real rate is zero over the savings period. A similar scheme applies to government bonds with initial maturities of three years or more.

[50]Open-market-type operations refer to the use of primary issues of securities through auctions of central bank or government deposits at the initiative of the central bank to influence monetary conditions in the financial markets.

[51]UCCs, RCCs, and small commercial banks were requested to deposit part of their free reserves in special deposits at the PBC. In 1994, a total of ¥ 14 billion was collected in one-year time deposits, yielding an interest rate of 12.6 percent. In this connection, the PBC's provincial branches were assigned quotas to be collected within their jurisdictions.

were introduced because the PBC had to find some means of coping with the excess liquidity until the infrastructure for open market operations was ready.

At the end of 1993, the PBC contemplated the introduction of genuine open market operations as its main instrument of monetary policy. Soon, however, the PBC realized that the absence of an integrated interbank market and interest liberalization were major obstacles to the effective conduct of open market operations. Nevertheless, it was considered that open market operations could be used to pursue purely quantitative adjustments in banks' reserves, rather than the more common combination of price and quantity adjustments used in a liberalized environment.

However, the authorities quickly realized that changing the volumes of reserves of the banking system (by injecting or absorbing liquidity) *without* affecting the interest rates could, in fact, induce additional instability in the system. For instance, through the action of the credit multiplier, an injection of liquidity could stimulate additional bank lending, leading to the creation of additional deposits, which could, in turn, further increase bank lending. Even though this process would eventually extinguish, it might lead to an overshooting of the central bank's initial targets, depending on the behavior of the multiplier, and could thus require additional interventions (in the opposite direction) by the central bank.

The authorities thus put on hold their plans to rely on open market operations. At the same time, they made additional efforts to develop an environment wherein the open market instrument could be used effectively, including through the gradual liberalization of interest rates (see Section IX). The preparations for open market operations included the issuance by the Ministry of Finance of six-month and one-year treasury bills in early 1994 (a project that was subsequently shelved because it proved premature) and again in late 1995, and the development of a provisional book-entry system (the Provisional Securities Settlement System) by the PBC.

Monetary Developments

Monetary developments since the start of the economic reforms have been characterized by wide fluctuations in the growth rates of money and credit aggregates, which is in line with the characteristic cycles through which the Chinese economy has been going. The nature of these cycles has been well documented in the literature on China.[52] This subsection concentrates on the monetary aspects of those cycles, analyzing the relationship and interactions between the instrument framework and monetary developments during the successive cycles.

Since 1979, China has gone through four macroeconomic cycles, the most recent of which has not yet been completed. A review of monetary developments in these four cycles brings to the surface inconsistencies between the monetary policy control framework and the developments in the financial sector, in addition to highlighting the handicaps that the PBC had to overcome in institution building during the first decade of its existence.

The First Cycle (1979–82)

The main engine of economic growth during the first cycle was agricultural reform—leading to a significant increase in rural incomes—and increases in domestic investment. Broad money grew by nearly 25 percent in the latter part of 1979 and most of 1980, and the annual inflation rate reached 20 percent during that same period. In 1981, price controls, direct credit controls, and trade policies were tightened in an effort to restore orderly conditions.

The Second Cycle (1984–Early 1986)

The second cycle was initiated with the introduction of a two-tier pricing system, the granting of greater autonomy to enterprises in setting wages, the liberalization of foreign trade, and the establishment of a two-tier banking system. However, increased investment spending and the large wage increases

---

[52]See Khor (1991) and Bell, Khor, and Kochhar (1993).

granted by many enterprises not confronted with hard budget constraints led to the overheating of the economy. Credit expanded from a 9 percent annualized growth rate at the beginning of 1984 to 76 percent in the fourth quarter of that year. Inflation went up to 17 percent in early 1985.

The second cycle was the first one in which the PBC operated as a "proper" central bank in a two-tier financial system. The problems encountered in controlling monetary developments may to a large extent be attributable to the central bank's—and, more generally, the authorities'—unfamiliarity with using monetary policy instruments other than credit quotas in the newly decentralized financial system. Even though reserve requirements had been introduced and the PBC was in a position to regulate its credit to the banking system, the main reply to the monetary overheating came through a stricter enforcement of the credit quotas in 1985. Additional measures consisted of raising the interest rates and devaluing the renminbi.

The Third Cycle (Mid-1986–Late 1989)

The third cycle originated in concerns about the slowdown in economic growth that resulted from the tightening of policies in 1985. Credit policy was eased in 1986; as described above, credit quotas for individual banks had become merely indicative, and banks had more freedom in setting their interest rates. In addition, regional interbank markets emerged. The combination of these measures and innovations fueled broad money and domestic credit growth to annual rates of over 30 percent (Chart 8).

The growth in these aggregates was largely brought about by a significant drawdown of the banks' reserves. As shown in Chart 9, at the end of 1985, total reserves were at 27 percent of bank deposits—compared with the required levels of 10 percent—and the more liberal application of credit quotas and the establishment of interbank markets instigated banks to use the reserves for additional lending. By the second quarter of 1988, total reserves had come down to 17 percent of total deposits—still several percentage points above the required minimum, which, in the process, had been raised to 13 percent.

These developments revealed some of the growing inconsistencies between the PBC's control framework and financial sector developments in the latter part of the 1980s. The relaxation of credit quotas could not be compensated for by a more active use of the PBC's other instruments: reserve requirements were increased on two occasions, but further increases would probably have hit banks that were suffering from liquidity shortages—liquidity was spread unevenly across the country—and would

Chart 8. Money, Credit, and Price Developments, 1985:IV–1994:III

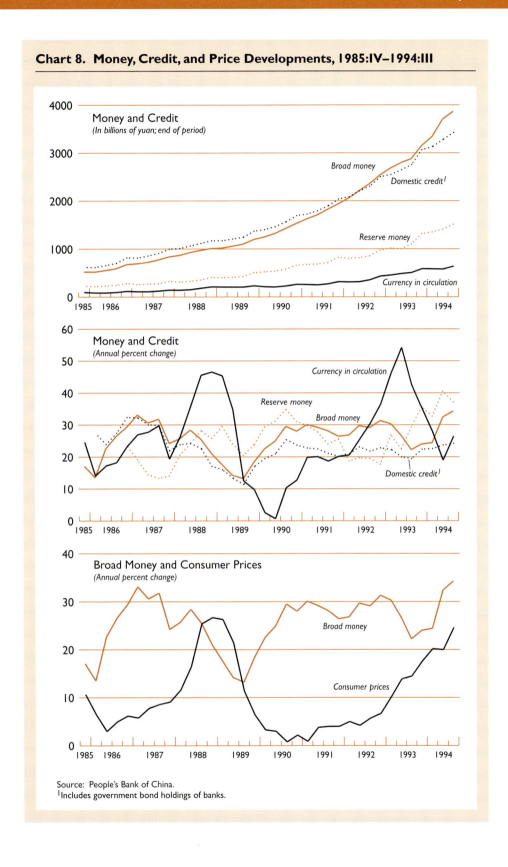

Money and Credit
(In billions of yuan; end of period)

Broad money

Domestic credit[1]

Reserve money

Currency in circulation

Money and Credit
(Annual percent change)

Currency in circulation

Reserve money

Broad money

Domestic credit[1]

Broad Money and Consumer Prices
(Annual percent change)

Broad money

Consumer prices

Source: People's Bank of China.
[1]Includes government bond holdings of banks.

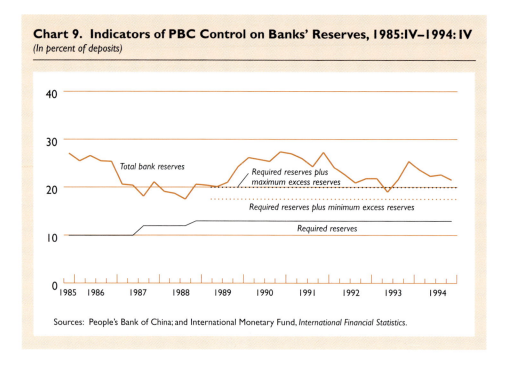

Chart 9. Indicators of PBC Control on Banks' Reserves, 1985:IV–1994:IV
(In percent of deposits)

Sources: People's Bank of China; and International Monetary Fund, *International Financial Statistics.*

have met with resistance from the political authorities, because such increases would have prevented the banks from fulfilling the credit plan objectives. Thus, even though the growth of PBC credit to the banks was drastically reduced in 1987 (Chart 10), the PBC had in general not enough freedom to use this instrument and effectively absorb the banks' excess reserves.

The PBC's control problems were further exacerbated by its institutional structure, a legacy of the past. Political decentralization had drastically altered the relationships between the PBC's branches and headquarters, on the one hand, and the local political authorities, specialized banks, and enterprises, on the other (Huang (1994)). Before the reforms, PBC branches were simply the executors of the credit plan in their political region.[53] Since the start of the reform process, however, they have been used as effective instruments in the promotion of local interests and economic growth. In fact, local political authorities considered PBC branches as merely departments of local governments that had to meet their objectives. The web of common interests among local authorities, SOEs, and specialized banks put local PBC branches under great pressure and pulled them away from the supervision and in-

fluence of the PBC headquarters. These factors made proper monetary and credit control very difficult.

After inflation had sharply climbed to an annual rate of more than 25 percent in 1988 (bottom panel, Chart 8), drastic measures to tighten credit policies, along with other economic policy measures, were taken. Credit quotas became mandatory again, the reserve ratio was increased to 13 percent, PBC credit was tightened, interest rate liberalization measures were reversed, interest rates were raised, interbank market activities were controlled more tightly, and the renminbi was devalued by 21 percent. The 1989 guidelines on excess reserve requirements (as discussed above) had the effect of absorbing the larger part of the banks' excess or free reserves (Chart 9).[54] Additional measures enacted in 1988 strengthened the PBC headquarters' control over the lending activities of its branches, imposed the requirement that appointments of branch presidents be approved by PBC headquarters, and ensured that PBC short-term lending to financial institutions would be reimbursed when it fell due.

As illustrated in the bottom panel of Chart 8, the growth of broad money fell from 27 percent in the second quarter of 1988 to 13 percent in the third quarter of 1989. Inflation started going down in the

---

[53]PBC branches had to follow strict rules and guidelines in implementing the credit plan, and Huang (1994) reports that strict discipline and punishments were imposed for failures to achieve the binding plans.

[54]In addition, however, as can be seen from Chart 9, the austerity measures led to the quick reconstitution of total reserves (to 25–30 percent of total deposits by mid-1990, similar to the level attained in 1985).

Chart 10. Factors Contributing to Changes in Banks' Reserves[1]
(Annual percent change)

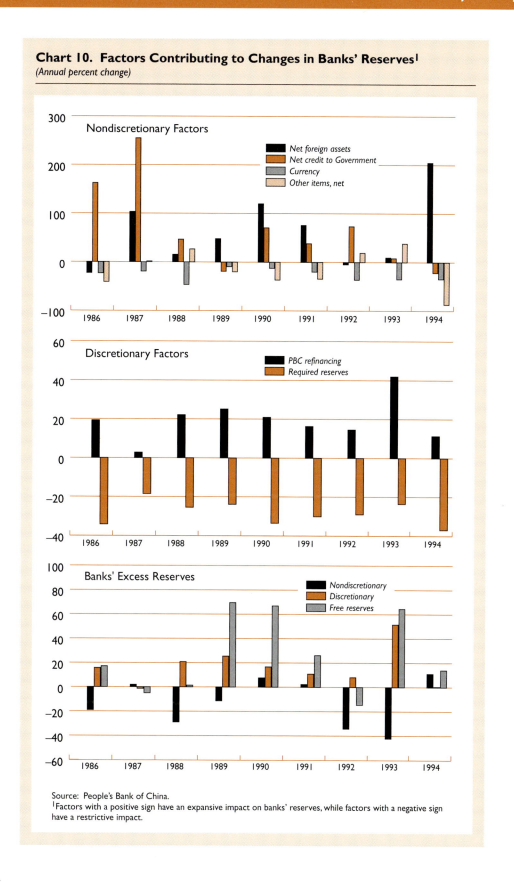

Source: People's Bank of China.
[1]Factors with a positive sign have an expansive impact on banks' reserves, while factors with a negative sign have a restrictive impact.

first quarter of 1989 and reached its lowest point (3 percent) in the third quarter of 1990, causing interest rates to become positive again in real terms.

The Fourth Cycle (1992–Present)

The fourth cycle has not yet come to an end. In late 1991, the domestic reform process, as well as the opening of the economy, resumed, including price reforms, the beginning of the reform of the SOEs, and the extension of Special Economic Zones to inland regions. Just as in earlier cycles, these reforms fueled an investment boom, accommodated by expansionary domestic financial policies. The sequencing of events in the fourth cycle is similar to the previous cycle, as growth in money and credit since late 1991 has for the greater part been financed through a drawdown of the banks' free reserves.

The growth of broad money oscillated around the 30 percent level in 1992. Inflation started picking up in the third quarter of 1992 and reached 20 percent at the end of 1993 (Chart 8, bottom panel). Measures to tighten credit were taken in the summer of 1993 as part of the 16-Point Program. These measures included increasing interest rates and tightening PBC credit to the banks (including through the centralization of PBC credit at the headquarters level), as well as recalling overdue PBC loans, recalling "illegal" loans made through the interbank market by banks and TICs, and taking measures to improve the authorities' control over the interbank market.

The credit crunch that followed the implementation of the program mainly hit the SOEs, which led the authorities to take accommodating actions toward the end of 1993. PBC credit to the banks had already picked up during the third quarter but grew even faster in the fourth quarter of 1993.

While monetary factors combined with a real estate boom were major factors behind the acceleration of inflation in 1993, the further acceleration in 1994 primarily stemmed from increases in food prices, adjustments in agricultural and other administered prices, and the reform of the exchange and tax system. In fact, monetary and credit policies were considerably tightened during 1994.

Despite this tightening, broad money grew rapidly (with 34 percent annual growth rate at the end of September 1994, compared with an annual growth of 24 percent in 1993). Growth in domestic credit also accelerated in 1994 from an annual rate of about 20 percent in 1993 to about 27 percent at the end of September (Chart 8). These higher growth rates reflect the large increase in PBC lending to the public sector at the end of 1993 and the increase in net foreign assets of the PBC in 1994 (Charts 10 and 11).

During most of 1994, the PBC tried to offset the expansionary effects of the movements in broad money and domestic credit by restricting its lending to the banking system, recalling loans from specialized banks, and attracting special deposits from selected financial institutions. The PBC's net foreign assets grew from ¥ 148.7 billion at the end of 1993 to ¥ 416.5 billion at the end of September 1994 (Chart 11), while its claims on financial institutions slightly decreased to ¥ 981.2 billion at the end of 1993, whereupon they started growing again, but at a more modest pace than in 1993.

Charts 10 and 11 draw a distinction between those items on the PBC's balance sheet that are under its control (discretionary factors) and those that are not (nondiscretionary factors). The charts show that in 1994 the PBC was able to offset the larger part of the increase in the nondiscretionary factors with two instruments, its lending and reserve requirements. As a result, as seen in the bottom panel of Chart 11, the banks' excess reserves increased only slightly (from ¥ 266 billion to ¥ 291 billion).[55] Although the banks' excess reserves remained above the PBC guidelines (5–7 percent of total deposits), the ratio of total reserves to deposits dropped from 25 percent at the end of 1993 to 22 percent at the end of September 1994 (Chart 9).

The parallel increase in banks' free reserves and in PBC refinancing during the second half of 1993 (as depicted in Chart 11) reveals in part some of the inefficiencies of the interbank market. Banks with shortages of reserves received additional PBC credit, while banks with surplus funds built up excess reserves. However, these developments also reveal differences in the ability of individual banks to manage their reserves. At the branch level, for instance, the quota of PBC credit obtained during the year from the head office is crucial, as it will set the basis for the next year's quota. In such a framework, excess reserves, which, in addition, are remunerated by the PBC, do not have much importance.

This latest cycle brings to the forefront another inconsistency between the control framework and the financial system. Several NBFIs have become increasingly active in banking operations. This activity helps explain why, particularly since 1990–91, total credit growth exceeded the targeted volumes. Since the early 1990s, growth in domestic credit—the concept covered by the credit plan—has increasingly deviated from growth in (net) domestic assets—the

---

[55]Excess reserves are defined here as the sum of the banks' required excess reserves (5–7 percent of their deposits to be held at the PBC) and any free reserves that they have over and above these required amounts (basically "free" deposits at the PBC and vault cash).

This analysis disregards the behavior of "other items, (net)" on the PBC's balance sheet. The erratic fluctuation of this aggregated component means that any attempt to analyze the sources of banks' reserves can only be approximate.

Chart 11. Sources of Banks' Reserves[1], 1985:IV–1994:IV
(In billions of yuan)

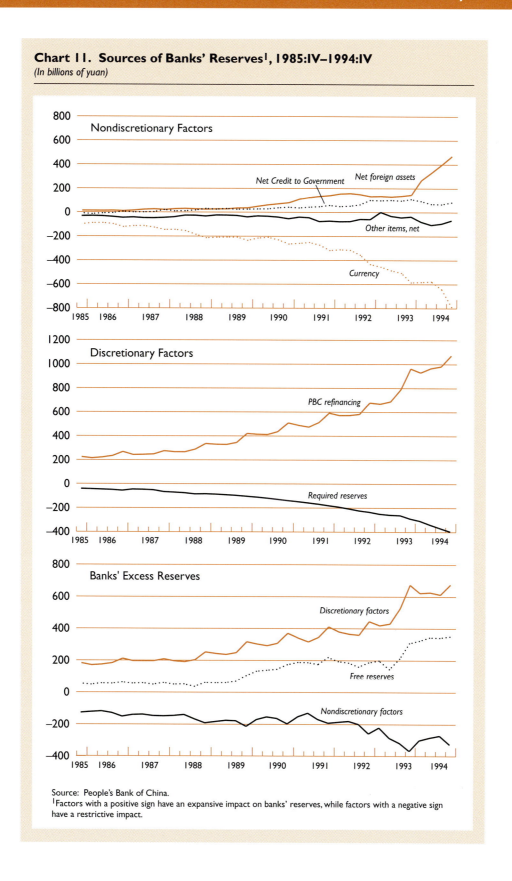

Source: People's Bank of China.

[1]Factors with a positive sign have an expansive impact on banks' reserves, while factors with a negative sign have a restrictive impact.

concept that includes credit to the economy granted by NBFIs. The PBC has tried to correct part of this problem by including several categories of NBFIs under the credit plan.

Overview: Monetary Developments Versus the Instrument Framework

This section has demonstrated that since 1985–86—the time of the introduction of new monetary policy instruments—monetary policy has been confronted with the dilemma that neither direct nor indirect instruments can operate fully effectively. Financial sector reform has gone far enough in terms of decentralization and diversification to make the "old-style" direct controls increasingly ineffective. At the same time, however, resort to indirect instruments has remained impaired because of three factors.

- The financial sector is not yet sufficiently developed to transmit the impulses given through these instruments to the rest of the economy. The large banks have a structural need for funds to fulfill the credit plan targets, the incentive structure for the banks to manage their funds more profitably remains poorly developed, and

the organization of the banks is not conducive to liquidity management and monitoring at the aggregate level.

- Because the interbank market is not yet nationally integrated, it cannot efficiently redistribute liquidity among the banks. Those with shortages must therefore seek accommodation at the PBC. This shortcoming also prevents the interbank market from efficiently transmitting monetary policy signals.
- The (political) requirements that steer the credit plan limit the PBC's control over its own balance sheet and, thus, its operational autonomy in using indirect levers to influence macroeconomic monetary conditions. More particularly, PBC lending to the banks remains dominated by the need to fill the banks' resource gap in order to meet the credit plan targets.

As a result of these transitional circumstances, indirect instruments have often been used as substitutes for the missing redistribution mechanisms needed to channel funds from banks (or regions) with surplus liquidity to those with shortages. In addition, during each episode of economic overheating in the 1980s, the central bank had to resort to direct administrative controls and—to a considerable extent—moral suasion to bring back orderly conditions.

VIII   Developments in the Exchange System

The Chinese exchange system has changed at an accelerating speed during the past fifteen years from one in which access to foreign exchange was highly restricted and the exchange rate was administered to a system wherein foreign exchange is available to bona fide buyers at a market-determined rate. Developments in the foreign exchange system were also characterized by initial local experiments that were in the process transplanted to the entire economy.

Early Stages: Regulated Exchange Rates and the Foreign Exchange Plan

When China assumed its seat on the Executive Board of the International Monetary Fund in 1980, the external value of the renminbi was linked to a basket of internationally traded currencies. The weights in the basket were based on the relative importance of currencies in China's external transactions and on the relative values of these currencies in international markets. All spot transactions were performed at the rates derived from the value of the basket, although rates for currencies other than the U.S. dollar were changed only when the calculated rate diverged from the previously published rate by 1 percent or more; for some other currencies, the incremental limit was lower. All spot transactions on a given day were performed at the published rates.

Foreign exchange transactions were usually based on a foreign exchange plan, prepared by various ministries. The Bank of China (BOC) was responsible for implementing the plan, and all transactions were performed in accordance with it. At the beginning of 1981, an internal settlement rate was introduced, at which all purchases of foreign exchange had to take place. All national enterprises engaged in foreign trade were required to execute their purchases of foreign exchange from the BOC at this rate. The rate was computed by adding an equalization price to the official rate. At the end of 1981, the official buying and selling rates were ¥ 1.7411 per U.S. dollar and ¥ 1.7499 per U.S. dollar, respectively. At the same time, the internal settlement rate was ¥ 2.8 per U.S. dollar. The official rate was used for non-trade-related transactions.

On January 1, 1981, an experimental trading system was established by the BOC in a few cities, such as Beijing, Guangzhou, Hefei, Shanghai, and Tianjing. Domestic enterprises that were permitted to retain foreign exchange in the form of retention quotas were permitted to sell this foreign exchange to other domestic enterprises authorized to buy it. The BOC acted as broker for these transactions and levied commissions of 0.1–0.3 percent on both sides of the transactions. The BOC did not trade in this system for its own account and was not permitted to assume foreign exchange positions. All these transactions were executed at the internal settlement rate of ¥ 2.8 per U.S. dollar. At an early stage, forward rates (which were not based on interest rate differentials) were also published for 15 currencies. It is not known to what extent transactions actually took place at these rates.

At the beginning of 1985, the use of the internal settlement rate was discontinued, and all transactions were to be executed at the official rate published by the State Administration for Exchange Control (SAEC), the agency charged with implementing and enforcing exchange regulations on behalf of the People's Bank of China (PBC). At the beginning of 1986, the exchange regime was changed from one of pegging to a basket to a system of managed floating.

Swap Centers and Retention Quotas: First Step Toward Market-Determined Rates

In November 1986, Chinese enterprises and foreign investment corporations in the four Special Economic Zones (SEZs) of Shantou, Shenzhen, Xiamen, and Zhuhai were permitted to transact foreign exchange in Foreign Exchange Adjustment Centers (FEACs) at rates agreed between buyers and sellers.[56] Initially, the trade volume in these so-called adjustment or swap centers was small. Trade took place at a

---

[56]See also Khor (1993) for an overview of the swap centers and their contribution to the economy.

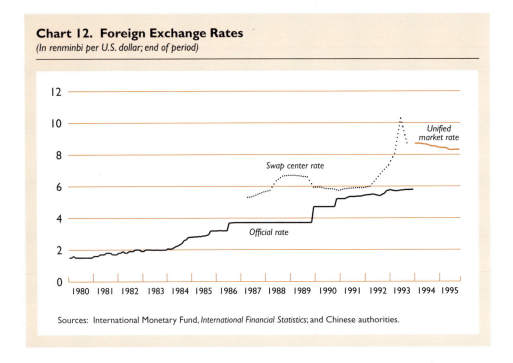

Chart 12. Foreign Exchange Rates
(In renminbi per U.S. dollar; end of period)

Sources: International Monetary Fund, *International Financial Statistics*; and Chinese authorities.

rate that was somewhat depreciated in relation to the official rate. In Shenzhen, for example, the exchange rate depreciated from ¥ 5.5 per U.S. dollar to about ¥ 6 per U.S. dollar during 1987 (Chart 12).

In early 1988, all domestic entities that were allowed to retain foreign exchange earnings were also allowed to trade in the centers, and, by October 1988, 80 swap centers had been established. The rate continued to depreciate in relation to the official rate. At the same time, foreign exchange retention quotas for enterprises in several industrial sectors and in some regions were liberalized.

The official exchange rate remained unchanged at ¥ 3.72 per U.S. dollar from July 5, 1986 to December 15, 1989, at which time a 21.2 percent depreciation of the renminbi was announced. At the end of 1989, the exchange rate of the renminbi against the U.S. dollar was 4.72. In the swap centers, the renminbi depreciated against the U.S. dollar from ¥ 5.25 in the first quarter of 1987 to ¥ 6.7 in the first half of 1989 before appreciating until reaching ¥ 5.4 per U.S. dollar by the end of 1989 (Chart 12).

In February 1989, regulations were issued by the SAEC regarding the use of foreign exchange purchased at swap centers. Imports of inputs for agriculture, textiles, and technologically advanced and light industries were to be given priority. Purchases of foreign exchange for a wide range of consumer goods were prohibited. Meanwhile, although the BOC was still China's specialized foreign exchange bank, an increasing number of other institutions were authorized by the SAEC to handle specific transactions. At the turn of the

decade, more than 100 institutions were authorized to handle various types of foreign exchange transactions.

The right to trade in retention quotas was extended in early 1988 to all domestic entities engaged in foreign trade, including those entities that were permitted to retain foreign exchange earnings. Private individuals were also permitted to purchase foreign exchange through authorized banks. The retention quota system is reviewed in Box 7.

Branches of the SAEC, operating on behalf of the associated branches of the PBC, intervened from time to time to stabilize prices in the swap centers. Decisions to intervene were taken locally at the branch level, independent of the SAEC and PBC headquarters. The foreign exchange used in these interventions was drawn from local stabilization funds that had been created through earlier purchases of foreign exchange and retention quotas in the local swap centers. The foreign exchange part of these stabilization funds was usually held by local branches of the BOC.

By the beginning of August 1992, some centers had fully computerized their dealing systems. The computer system simulated a typical "open outcry" arrangement.[57] At other centers, participants

---

[57]In an open outcry arrangement, buyers and sellers enter their bids and offers on computer terminals that are networked. Members can enter only what they have customer orders for, but they are not compelled to do so, and they can choose at what time during the session they make the entries. Entries can also be changed at any time. All participants (and observers) can see the entries made by the other participants on their screens, as well as on a large wall screen. Each bid or offer is identified by dealer. Clients

Box 7. The Retention Quota System

Under the retention quota system, China maintained a multiple exchange arrangement. An administered official exchange rate was used for the foreign exchange plan, the surrender of foreign exchange, and the purchase of foreign exchange with retention quotas. However, the actual effective exchange rate received when surrendering foreign exchange or paid when acquiring foreign exchange depended on the quota and cash retention systems. The retention quota rate and the cash exchange rate usually were different from the official exchange rate. These rates could also diverge substantially among centers in different parts of the country.

Under the retention quota system, Chinese enterprises were required to surrender their foreign exchange to authorized banks for renminbi at the official exchange rate. These enterprises were then allocated a certain percentage of surrendered foreign exchange in the form of retention quotas. Foreign-funded enterprises (FFEs) could choose whether to retain foreign exchange or receive retention quotas. The quota retention account was a book entry, denominated in U.S. dollar, that showed the holder's right to purchase foreign exchange at the official exchange rate for approved imports or debt service, up to the amount in the account. Retention quotas were usually approved automatically for payments under the trade plan; they were granted for imports over and above the plan with the approval of the State Planning Commission and the Ministry of Foreign Economic Relations and Trade (MOFERT). Retention quotas had no fixed maturity, and they could be traded at prices reflecting supply and demand throughout the swap centers.

On the presentation of evidence of the surrender of foreign exchange, MOFERT verified the amount of retention quotas to which an enterprise was entitled, as well as the percentage distribution of retention quotas to the state, the local authorities, and foreign trade companies. The percentages were predetermined by the State Council and varied by commodity and over time. In 1992, part of the retention quotas made available to the state were purchased at a premium equal to the monthly weighted average of the rate in the swap market.[1] As a consequence, the actual effective exchange rate for the conversion of export proceeds into renminbi was a weighted average of the official and swap market exchange rates, which varied by commodity and over time. FFEs (wholly foreign owned and joint ventures) were permitted to retain all of their export earnings and to transact the foreign exchange in the swap centers. Retained foreign exchange had to be deposited in accounts with one of the authorized banks.

On an experimental basis, Chinese enterprises in Shanghai and some other coastal regions were also permitted to retain the same percentage of foreign exchange as they would have received in quotas. Retained foreign exchange could be purchased and sold through the swap centers by these enterprises. Authorized banks could, without additional approval by the State Administration for Exchange Control (SAEC), inititate import payments directly using the retained foreign exchange when presented by these enterprises with import authorizations from MOFERT. These Chinese enterprises could continue to use their accumulated retention quotas but could not receive additional quotas. This cash retention scheme did not extend to local authorities.

Using the retention quota system, an exporter of general commodities initially received 100 percent in renminbi at the official rate for a surrender of 100 percent of foreign exchange. At the same time, the exporter also received—and could retain or sell in the swap market—retention quotas equivalent to 40 percent of the foreign exchange surrendered. The remaining 60 percent of retention quotas were allocated directly by the SAEC in the following way:

- Retention quotas equivalent to 30 percent of the total were purchased by the PBC at the prevailing swap market rate for quotas. The renminbi proceeds of this purchase were transferred to the exporter's renminbi account.
- Retention quotas equivalent to 20 percent were credited to the Central Government's quota account.
- Retention quotas equivalent to 10 percent were credited to the local authorities' quota account.

The exporter, therefore, was effectively reimbursed at the swap market rate for 70 percent of export proceeds, either in the form of the official rate plus quotas (40 percent of the proceeds) or in the form of the official rate plus allocation and resale of quotas at the market rate (30 percent of the proceeds).[2]

As of July 1, 1992, the PBC started selling the quotas that it had bought at the market rate to importers through the swap market at the prevailing swap market rate. As a result, the Government's access to foreign exchange at the official rate fell from 50 percent to 20 percent.

_____

[1]Retention quotas made available to local authorities were puchased at the official exchange rate.

_____

[2]This example of an exporter of general commodities would have applied to 70–80 percent of exports; foreign-owned and joint-venture enterprises could retain 100 percent of export proceeds in cash.

may watch the proceedings from behind a barrier and pass instructions to their brokers. Brokers also stay in touch with their clients through telephones. In the Chinese version of this arrangement, there were 60 dealing positions, but only a fraction of the capacity was used on a typical day.

watched bids and offers placed on a large screen. Effectively, there was not much difference between dealing under these two arrangements. Bids and offers were matched on the basis of price and time.[58] Dealing ended when no matching orders to buy and sell were entered on the system within a 30-second period. There was no interference by authorities in the pricing or dealing process.

Settlement Procedures

The buying and selling of retention quotas and foreign exchange were conducted through the accounts of the swap centers. On the day of the trade, the buyers and sellers made transfers to the swap center: buyers transferred the renminbi counterpart and sellers the retention quotas or the foreign exchange. In some centers, the renminbi accounts of the sellers and the quota or foreign exchange accounts of the buyers were credited on the next day. A penalty of 0.003 percent a day was charged for any unsettled amounts. In still other centers, the accounts of local customers were credited on the second day after trading; the crediting of the accounts of customers from outside the center could take up to one week.

Regulation of Swap Center Trading

Initially, there were no generally applicable regulations for the swap centers, as each center issued or applied its own variety of regulations. Effective April 14, 1993, the SAEC sought to rectify this situation by issuing operational regulations for the swap centers. The explicitly stated main purpose of these new regulations was to promote flows or arbitrage between centers. Another important provision explicitly forbade transactions bypassing the swap markets. The SAEC at this time also had the power to control market access on the basis of a "guiding priority list." Trading arrangements in the swap centers are reviewed in Box 8.

The volume of turnover grew by some 30–40 percent annually over the five years up to 1992, when turnover reached $25 billion. However, growth was much slower in 1993. In that year, the market developed in distinctly different phases. January and most of February were still characterized by expansive economic policies and a rapidly growing economy,

and demand for foreign exchange increased rapidly as a result of the boom in investments and imports. The swap rate continued to rise throughout most of this period, from some ¥ 7.0 per U.S. dollar in early January to about ¥ 8.4 in the third week of February. The continued depreciation of the renminbi in the swap markets led in late February to the imposition of an administrative cap by the SAEC on the swap rate at about ¥ 8.2 per U.S. dollar, in an apparent contradiction of the swap market regulations. This cap remained in place until the end of May. During this period, most sellers withdrew from the market, and turnover fell sharply. Instead, black market activity intensified, and the rate in that market depreciated to about ¥ 11.0 per U.S. dollar. The swap rate hovered around ¥ 8.0 in most centers.

The next stage in swap center trading in 1993 began with the lifting of the cap on the swap rate on June 1. Following the lifting of the cap, the swap rate depreciated almost immediately to about ¥ 10.0 per U.S. dollar; for the rest of June, the rate remained about ¥ 10.5 per U.S. dollar in most centers, close to the black market rate. The last stage of development during this rather unsettling year began with the announcement of a tightening of financial policies at the beginning of July. The appointment of a new governor of the PBC also raised strong expectations in the market of a change in policies. Therefore, the PBC intervention in the swap markets on July 5, 1993 had a powerful impact on rates. In one week, the renminbi appreciated from about ¥ 10.7 per U.S. dollar to ¥ 8.5 per U.S. dollar. The mood in the market was positive, reinforced by expectations of further changes in emphasis in policy implementation. Public statements were made by PBC officials to the effect that the renminbi exchange rates would be unified within five years. However, there was no observable convergence of swap rates among the different centers in 1993, and arbitraging the differences remained difficult or impossible despite the regulations intended to facilitate this.

Reform Plans and Reforms Since 1993

Reform Plans

In March 1993, the State Council decided that the SAEC should function under the leadership of the PBC. As a result, the SAEC no longer reports directly to the State Council but through the PBC. The potential for conflicting or overlapping functions and measures in foreign exchange matters between these two bodies has thus been reduced.

The major concern of the Chinese authorities continued to be the divergence of rates among the different swap centers and the difficulty of arbitraging

---

[58]Lower-priced selling orders had priority over higher-priced selling orders; higher-priced buying orders had priority over lower-priced buying orders. For orders at the same price, priority was based on time of data entry; early entry had priority over late entry. The computer system identified the lowest-selling and highest-buying orders that could be matched and highlighted them on the screens for 30 seconds. If neither party wished to change its orders, or if no orders at a better price were submitted within the 30 seconds, the deal was struck. A digital clock on the screens showed the time remaining of the 30-second period. Deals done were also shown cumulatively on the screens, together with information about prices. Deals were struck throughout the trading day in this manner, as dealers adjusted their prices on the basis of their objectives and the observed transactions.

Box 8. Trading Arrangements in Swap Centers

The regulations governing the operation of Foreign Exchange Adjustment Centers (FEACs) were determined by local branches of the State Administration for Exchange Control (SAEC) and varied from one center to another. Typically, a transactor in the swap center needed the approval of the local branch of the SAEC organizing the center. This approval was granted automatically to members of the exchange. An agent who wished to trade in an FEAC other than the local designated center needed the approval of the SAEC that organized the local center; the Shanghai SAEC, however, granted this approval automatically. Quota accounts that were traded in FEACs had to be held with the local SAEC organizing the center. Therefore, sellers of quota accounts from outside the local area had to transfer their quota accounts in advance to the SAEC organizing the center.

A swap center would typically be used by brokers, jobbers, and dealers. However, depending on the location of the center, their functions could be different.

Brokers were financial institutions authorized to deal in foreign exchange by the SAEC. The brokers acted only as agents and were not permitted to transact for their own accounts.

Jobbers were foreign trade and joint-venture companies with large volumes and frequent exchange transactions. In some centers, they were known as *dealers*. These jobbers/dealers were allowed only to trade for their own accounts.

In a special arrangement, 46 dealers represented local FEACs in the National Foreign Exchange Adjustment Center (NFEAC) in Beijing. These dealers traded only on behalf of the local FEACs and not on behalf of specific customers. The dealers could also send their orders to the NFEAC through brokers. The 46 FEACs covered all provinces and important cities; other FEACs could send orders indirectly to the NFEAC by passing their orders to one of the 46 FEACs represented on the NFEAC. The purpose of this arrangement was to create a channel for redistributing funds among centers; as a practical matter, however, it was rarely utilized.

A fixed commission of 0.15 percent was paid on each transaction by both buyers and sellers in both exchanges. Part of this amount (one third in the case of the NFEAC) was returned to the brokers, and members charged no additional fees to their customers. Trading hours varied but were usually in the morning. In the more active centers, trading hours were eventually extended until the end of the day.

---

these divergences. The answer to this problem was therefore seen as the integration of the regional markets into one national foreign exchange market. With this integration, the difference between the official and swap exchange rates would be reduced, and exchange rates would be unified within five years. After the unification of the exchange rates, the PBC would establish a central target or reference rate. The SAEC would intervene, when necessary, to keep the market rate within a predetermined range in relation to the reference rate.

The integration of regional markets was needed to achieve two goals. First, the flow and allocation of foreign exchange funds among regions was to be promoted through the market mechanism. Second, in order for the authorities to be able to intervene effectively in exchange markets, there should be a single observable exchange rate in the market, as intervention is very difficult when centers' rates diverge.

To achieve this integration of markets, all regional swap markets were to be amalgamated into a single center, located in Shanghai. This city was seen as the natural center, as it was at the leading edge of economic and financial development in China and the authorities foresaw that it eventually would evolve into an international financial center. The organization that was to handle this single market was to be called the China Foreign Exchange Trade System (CFETS). The regional swap markets would be branches of Shanghai's swap center. The SAEC headquarters in Beijing would set the operational rules for the market and advise on policy, while market interventions would take place in Shanghai. This plan was developed by the SAEC and approved by the PBC. As the old telecommunications infrastructure in China would not have been able to accommodate this kind of arrangement, it was envisaged that the regional swap centers would be linked to the market in Shanghai via satellite. The satellite network would be used for quotations, information, and renminbi settlements.

The market would continue to be based on the electronic trading system already employed by the more advanced swap centers, in which priority in transactions is given to price and time. In these centers, as explained above in footnote 58, a higher buying price has preference over a lower one, and a lower selling price over a higher one. Earlier price quotations have preference over later ones. In the envisaged integrated system, bids and offers would be submitted only to the Shanghai market, and local dealing would be neither permitted nor possible. Buyers and sellers in centers outside Shanghai would be linked electronically on-line to the Shanghai market. Information about rates and transactions would be fed back to the regional centers, where buyers and sellers would have the same information as if they were physically present in Shanghai. There would be no control in the system over deals between licensed participants, and deals could be struck between counterparts in different parts of the country.

To minimize interregional settlement flows, each regional center would at settlement first net the renminbi leg of all transactions at a given price for that region. The net outstanding at that price level would then be settled with the Shanghai center, which would become a counterpart to each transaction and the clearing center for the market. To protect the Shanghai center from the risk of settlement failures, foreign exchange funds to be sold would be credited to the center's foreign exchange account before being offered for sale on the market.

Only the Shanghai center would hold accounts abroad. All payments of foreign exchange to and from customers' foreign accounts would be effected through the Shanghai center's foreign accounts. The satellite network would be used only to carry information to domestic buyers and sellers about foreign exchange payments, while actual settlement would take place through transfers between foreign accounts. The Shanghai center's foreign accounts would legally be part of the PBC's balance sheet. Renminbi settlements and transfers of quotas were to take place over the satellite network.

The integration of the regional markets was to be implemented in three stages. First, 18 swap centers that already employed the electronic trading system would be linked to the Shanghai center by June 1994. These centers covered some 70 percent of the total swap market. The communications and computer system for operating the Shanghai exchange would have a parallel backup system in Shanghai, as well as a second backup in Beijing. Second, an additional 18 centers would be linked to Shanghai by the end of 1994. It was envisaged that by that time all major provinces, municipalities, and economic zones would be connected to the market. Third, another 34 centers would be added by June 1995, after which 70 centers, accounting for 95 percent of transactions, would be connected to the market, effectively creating a single national exchange market.

No transactions were to be permitted outside the swap centers, although such a rule might not be fully enforceable. Trading would initially take place in both cash and quotas, although it was foreseen that quotas would soon be phased out. Forward transactions would also be developed. Banks would in the future be permitted to deal for their own accounts.

Implementation

As it turned out, progress on these issues was much faster than had been foreseen only six months

earlier. On January 1, 1994, the official and swap market exchange rates were unified at the prevailing swap market exchange rate; the issuance of retention quotas was terminated, and it was decreed that outstanding quotas could be converted at the end-1993 official rate until the end of 1994; the priority lists that governed the provision of foreign exchange and regulated market access were abolished; and the requirement to obtain prior approval from the SAEC for the purchase of foreign exchange for most trade and trade-related transactions conducted by domestic enterprises was rescinded. On April 1, 1994, the CFETS became operational, creating an integrated system of foreign exchange trading centralized in Shanghai. The system is fully computerized, and all 24 major regional trading centers have been linked to the center through satellite and land-based connections. The CFETS offers, as planned, trading and settlement services to its members, which comprise domestic banks (both head offices and branches can be members), foreign banks, and a number of nonbank financial institutions (NBFIs). Trading is primarily conducted in renminbi against the U.S. dollar, although the renminbi is also traded against the Hong Kong dollar and—more recently—the Japanese yen. The 24 regional trading centers (including Shanghai) represent 90 percent of foreign currency trading in China. The CFETS represents the wholesale part of the foreign exchange market in China. It can be regarded as an interbank market in the sense that most of the participants are banks, although they do not trade directly with each other as in a conventional interbank market.

Trading is fully computerized and carried out through computer terminals connected to the CFETS in the regional centers. Members have no trading facilities in their own offices.[59] Once a bid and an offer have been matched, the CFETS becomes the counterpart to the trade and assumes responsibility for settlement. Buyers and sellers thus do not know with whom their bids or offers were originally matched.[60] Settlement takes place on the following business day. The CFETS (essentially, the PBC), by assuming responsibility for settlement, also assumes the credit risk of each transaction. So far, there have been only short delays—at most of a few days—in settlements, owing to human errors or technical problems. For the purpose of enforcing proper settlement procedures, the SAEC has the authority to impose penalties on members that fail to meet their payment com-

---

[59]From the market participants' point of view, they have only one counterpart in the market, the CFETS. The normal evaluation of counterpart risks and credit limits has no practical role in the current system, which is totally impersonal, providing no information to participants about the identity of other market participants.

[60]During the sessions, therefore, it is difficult or impossible for banks to monitor and control the operations of their traders.

mitments, and, in serious cases, the SAEC may terminate membership. No funds have been set aside to cover the potential losses associated with possible payment defaults.

Turnover in the CFETS market has averaged over $200 million a day. Although many domestic and foreign financial institutions, including the specialized banks, about 10 provincial banks, more than 100 foreign banks, and about 300 NBFIs, are authorized to deal in foreign exchange, the market is nonetheless dominated by one single bank, the BOC. By virtue of its size, and because only two of its branches have dealing rights, the BOC internally nets a large number of transactions that thus never enter the market.

Foreign exchange transactions conducted through centers not linked to the CFETS use the reference rate of the previous day, with no margins applied. The local SAEC branch stands ready to absorb excess supply or demand at the reference rate while covering itself through the CFETS.

Current regulations do not prohibit forward transactions involving the renminbi and the U.S. dollar, but no forward trading involving these two currencies has taken place so far. This lack of activity may be due to the remarkable stability of the exchange rate, which has steadily appreciated by some 3 percent since late 1994. Earlier, also, there was no domestic money market to help banks determine their marginal cost of domestic funds. The recently emerging domestic interbank market may support the hedging of forward operations; it is not clear, however, whether banks would be free to engage in hedging operations in foreign money markets.

The Present Exchange System

Domestic and Foreign-Funded Enterprises (FFEs)

Domestic enterprises are required to conduct their sales and purchases of foreign currency through authorized financial institutions. The exchange rates used by the banks for purchases and sales of foreign currencies have to be within a maximum spread of ±0.25 percent of the previous day's reference exchange rate, as published by the PBC (the weighted average of the previous day's CFETS transactions). Thus, domestic enterprises cannot buy or sell foreign exchange at that day's current market exchange rates. Exchange controls for bona fide current transactions are delegated to the banks, and purchases of foreign exchange by domestic enterprises require no prior approvals from the SAEC; banks verify the nature of the transactions on the basis of documents provided by the enterprises.

FFEs are allowed to retain up to 100 percent of their foreign currency receipts without time limit on foreign currency accounts with banks in China. They may also purchase or sell foreign exchange directly from the CFETS and are thus able to deal at current market exchange rates. These enterprises may also, if they choose to do so, deal through banks and receive treatment identical to domestic enterprises. Earlier, FFEs had to apply for approval of each transaction; however, this rule was simplified in 1995, and FFEs need only submit an annual foreign exchange plan. Within the scope of this plan (once it has been approved by the authorities), FFEs are free to enter the foreign exchange market.

Domestic enterprises are charged up to a 0.25 percent spread for foreign exchange purchases from banks, while FFEs pay only a 0.15 percent fee for their transactions through the CFETS. The settlement period is also different for domestic enterprises and FFEs. When transactions are conducted through the retail market (with banks), settlement takes place on the same day, while transactions of FFEs through the CFETS are settled on the following business day.

Domestic and Foreign Banks

In China's foreign exchange market, different regulations also apply to domestic and foreign banks. Domestic banks may both buy and sell foreign exchange for their customers, but foreign banks may only sell foreign currencies against the renminbi in the CFETS market (these banks' renminbi accounts are maintained with the PBC). However, this limitation does not apply to transactions of foreign banks on behalf of FFEs. Foreign banks are not allowed to operate in the domestic money market.

The cost of transacting in the CFETS market depends on the nature of the foreign currency transaction. When a designated bank buys or sells foreign exchange in the market for its own account, the bank is charged a 0.03 percent commission, while transactions on behalf of customers are charged a 0.15 percent commission. Two thirds of the revenue from such a commission goes to the CFETS, and one third to the bank.

The wholesale market does not provide for direct dealing between banks, and market making—two-way quotations to other dealers—is presently not possible. Transactions between the CFETS and banks (wholesale market) are settled differently than transactions between bank customers (the retail market). While wholesale market transactions are settled on the next business day, retail market transactions are settled on the same day. Because of this unusual feature, retail transactions have a shorter settlement period than wholesale transactions. Banks therefore cannot cover their retail transactions in the wholesale market on the same day, which is the way that markets normally function. This difference in settlement practices also makes efficient position and risk management in banks difficult. Banks have to hold liquid funds idle to meet the unforeseen contingencies arising from retail transactions, which effectively forces them to assume a foreign exchange risk position. In addition, foreign banks are limited to performing foreign exchange transactions for the accounts of FFEs, which usually are sellers in the market.

Domestic banks are required to hold a minimum amount of liquid foreign exchange assets to ensure that they have adequate liquidity to meet their obligations in foreign currencies. Banks have to cover any shortfalls in these funds on the next day; however, if foreign exchange holdings exceed the limit, banks are supposed to sell the excess in the CFETS market. The liquidity limit does not apply to foreign banks and NBFIs. There are no other limits that regulate the foreign exchange positions of these institutions.

Interventions by the PBC

The PBC is committed to maintaining a stable exchange rate in the foreign exchange market through interventions in the CFETS aimed at containing the appreciation of the exchange rate. The interventions, which are carried out in Shanghai, are triggered by deviations of the exchange rate of the renminbi against the U.S. dollar in the CFETS market during trading hours (a ±0.3 percent day-to-day fluctuation margin is allowed).[61] The need for interventions in the foreign exchange market during the following day is estimated on the basis of information about banks' purchases and sales of foreign exchange in customer transactions. Because the PBC is an ordinary member of the CFETS, other market participants do not know when the central bank is active in the market.

Prudential Regulation

Effective July 1, 1993, instructions were issued by the SAEC to banks and NBFIs on licensing, capital requirements, operational and control practices, and risk limits in foreign exchange operations. These regulations are based on old accounting concepts that require a complete separation of renminbi and foreign exchange capital and business. Therefore, while they oblige banks to follow prudent operational and control procedures, they are not applicable to risk management in an environment in which banks adopt international accounting practices. Neither can they be applied to foreign banks in China, if and

when these are authorized to engage in renminbi operations. In the present environment, therefore, banks are subject to unmonitored exchange rate risks.

Current regulations provide for licensing of foreign exchange operations, general prudential regulation, including on-site inspections by the SAEC of banks' and NBFIs' foreign-currency-denominated assets and liabilities, and reporting to the SAEC. Under these regulations, which cover Chinese financial institutions' foreign currency operations only in China, foreign exchange business and transactions are treated almost as if they were performed by separate institutions. Foreign-owned financial institutions' operations in China, as well as Chinese financial institutions' branches and subsidiaries abroad, are regulated by the PBC.

Although all the regulations entered into force as of July 1, 1993, they have been implemented only gradually. This situation could create problems if a legal dispute about the status and enforceability of the regulations were to arise. Taken together, however, the regulations represent a major step toward introducing modern prudential regulatory principles into Chinese banking, even though the regulations unfortunately cover only foreign exchange operations. The one critical element lacking in these regulations is a limitation of exposure to exchange rate risk.

Under the regulations, a bank's foreign exchange business must be completely separated from its domestic currency business, it must have capital in foreign exchange, and it must comply with prudential rules based on its foreign-currency-denominated assets and liabilities only. Profits and risks are also measured in foreign currency, usually U.S. dollars. The SAEC regulations apply only to Chinese-owned institutions operating in China. Foreign financial institutions in China are jointly supervised by the PBC and the authorities of the home country. Branches of Chinese financial institutions established outside the country are regulated by the PBC, while the foreign exchange activities of the head office and domestic branches of these institutions are regulated by the SAEC. Close cooperation between the two supervisory institutions is therefore required.

The status of bank branches has also in a broader sense been an important element in the evolution of the financial system in China. As pointed out in Section III, branches of financial institutions used to enjoy such a high level of autonomy that, although they appeared to be slightly less independent than fully owned subsidiaries, they did not easily fit the definition of bank branches as understood in industrial countries. The new commercial banking law should normalize that situation.

Under the new regulations, capital denominated and paid up in foreign exchange is required before any financial institution can engage in foreign ex-

---

[61]If larger changes in the daily rate were allowed, arbitrage opportunities might arise between the CFETS and retail markets.

change transactions. This requirement establishes a minimum capital base, which will expand subsequently in two ways. First, a mandatory reserve has to be built up with the after-tax profit. At least 50 percent of this profit must be set aside until the total of capital and reserves equals three times the minimum capital. Even after this requirement has been met, at least 10 percent of the profit must still be set aside in the reserve, which may subsequently be incorporated into the capital. Second, capital is built up through a prudential ratio in the regulations requiring the foreign capital base to be equal to at least 8 percent of foreign currency assets. The foreign exchange capital may be denominated and paid in any foreign currency, but the minimum required is expressed in U.S. dollars.

IX The Agenda for Developing a Market-Based Monetary and Exchange System

This section discusses the agenda for further financial reform in China toward a fully market-based system. It starts with a brief assessment of the achievements against which the thrust of the agenda can be gauged in the subsequent subsections. Reference is made to the decision of the Third Plenum in March 1993, which set out a blueprint for reforms during the remainder of this century (Box 1), and the section measures the progress of the reform program against that decision, describing options, possible alternatives, and potential pitfalls for the reform program.

Assessment of Achievements and Directions for Future Reform

Assessment

Section II has referred to the triangle of institutions, instruments, and markets as a useful tool for analyzing financial sector development. Sections III through VIII have presented a detailed account of the developments in various segments of China's financial sector. A summary overview of China's achievements thus far along the three axes is presented in Chart 13. The chart demonstrates the emphasis on institutional development in general and on the simultaneous development of institutions and markets in the foreign exchange system and the capital markets. By the same token, it indicates that the major efforts for the near future lie in further developing markets and instruments to complete the market-based character of the financial system. Further institution building is also required, even though several projects, such as the payments, clearing, and settlement system, are already well under way.

The perceived discrepancy between the well-advanced institution building and the less-advanced development of markets and instruments has its origin in two main factors: (i) the starting position of the Chinese financial sector at the beginning of the reforms; and (ii) the preference for an intermediate macroeconomic control mechanism in which the interventionist strategy continued to dominate de facto.

With respect to the first factor, the financial industry, unlike other sectors of the Chinese economy, was nonexistent when the reforms started. Institution building thus received priority treatment through the establishment of a two-tier banking system: the licensing of new banks, including branches of foreign banks; the emergence of a sector of nonbank financial institutions (NBFIs); and attempts to enhance the payments and settlement system.

This financial sector could gradually have been allowed to operate more in a market-oriented way; however, this did not happen because of the second factor, the authorities' preference for an interventionist strategy. The lack of equal progress in developing markets (and instruments, to a lesser extent) seems to reflect the authorities' preference for, and reliance on, an intermediate macroeconomic control mechanism. The monetary sector, in particular, was the focus of this control mechanism, in which control techniques of a planned economy continued to dominate de facto and market-based techniques operated only in a complementary role. This outcome stemmed from the authorities' desire to use the newly established financial sector as long as possible as the main vehicle for their economic development strategy and from the lack of market mechanisms in the state-owned enterprise (SOE) sector.

The decision of the Third Plenum implicitly recognized that the imbalance between institution building and market liberalization in the financial system, if protracted, could impede the further liberalization of the economy. Thus, the logical next step, as set out in the decision, was to put the creation of efficient markets at the heart of the reform strategy.

The picture presented above also explains why further reforms in China can now—more than in the first 15 rather unique years of reform—benefit from the experiences of other countries that liberalized their financial system and adopted market-based monetary policy techniques. China's financial system has arrived at that juncture where liberal-

Chart 13. Achievements in Financial Sector Development (Institutions, Markets, and Instruments) and Agenda for the Future

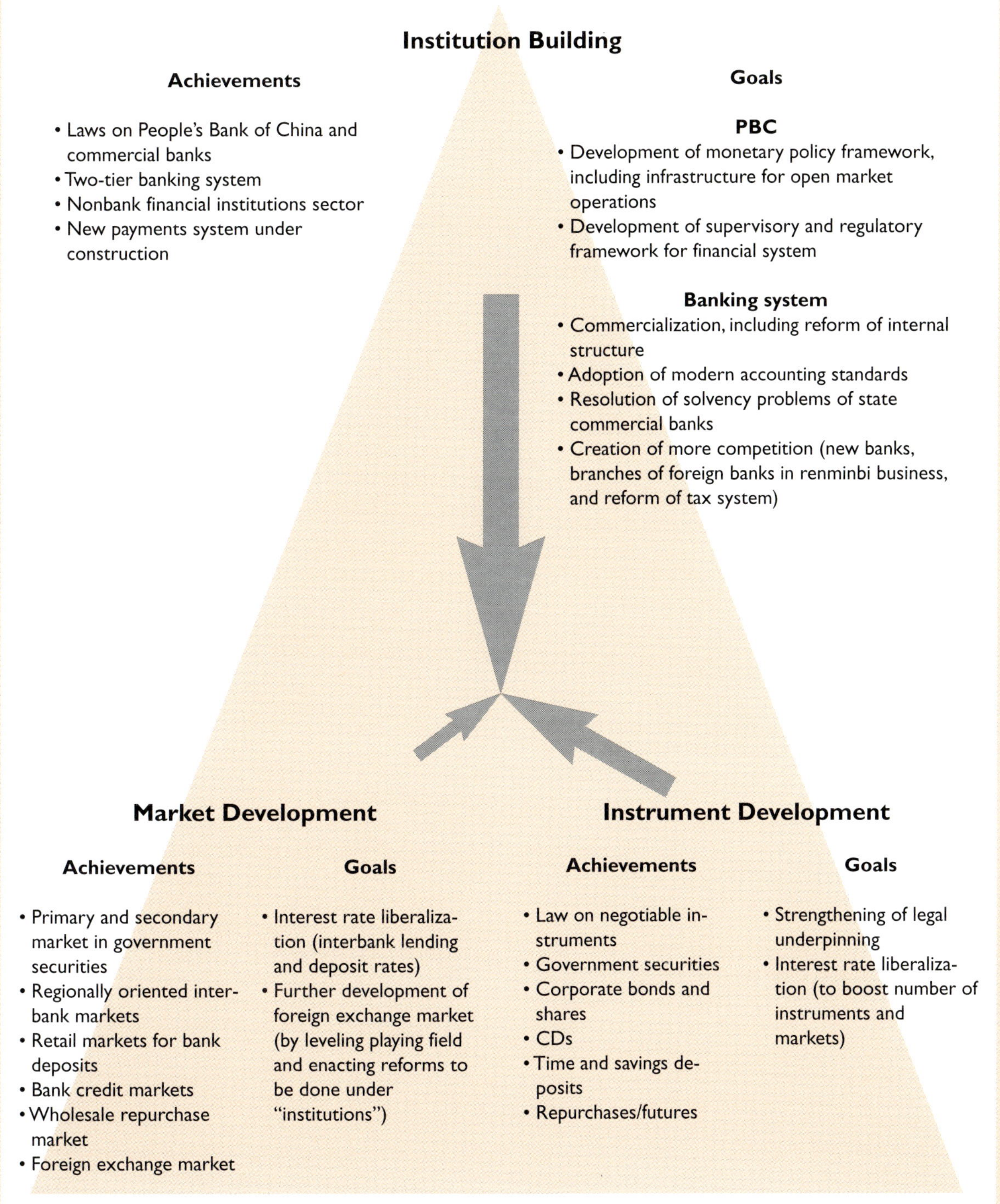

Institution Building

Achievements

- Laws on People's Bank of China and commercial banks
- Two-tier banking system
- Nonbank financial institutions sector
- New payments system under construction

Goals

PBC
- Development of monetary policy framework, including infrastructure for open market operations
- Development of supervisory and regulatory framework for financial system

Banking system
- Commercialization, including reform of internal structure
- Adoption of modern accounting standards
- Resolution of solvency problems of state commercial banks
- Creation of more competition (new banks, branches of foreign banks in renminbi business, and reform of tax system)

Market Development

Achievements

- Primary and secondary market in government securities
- Regionally oriented interbank markets
- Retail markets for bank deposits
- Bank credit markets
- Wholesale repurchase market
- Foreign exchange market

Goals

- Interest rate liberalization (interbank lending and deposit rates)
- Further development of foreign exchange market (by leveling playing field and enacting reforms to be done under "institutions")

Instrument Development

Achievements

- Law on negotiable instruments
- Government securities
- Corporate bonds and shares
- CDs
- Time and savings deposits
- Repurchases/futures

Goals

- Strengthening of legal underpinning
- Interest rate liberalization (to boost number of instruments and markets)

ization will need the most attention. Issues familiar to many countries in similar circumstances, including money market development, interest rate liberalization, bank restructuring, and the need for effective bank supervision and regulation, are in the spotlight.

Some General Principles

In order to put the future financial reform program in a broader context and before discussing specific issues, it is imperative to note those general principles regarding liberalization strategies that have emerged from the experience of other countries. To avoid major pitfalls while moving toward a predominantly market-based financial system relying on indirect instruments of monetary policy and, thus, to limit the cost associated with the transition that lies still ahead, a set of *concomitant and mutually reinforcing* reform measures has to be considered. Country experience (Alexander and others (1995)) indicates the need to take a number of actions:

- Insulate monetary policy from deficit financing. Large fiscal deficits, often accompanied by unlimited monetary financing of these deficits, generally put monetary policy objectives under strain and reduce the effectiveness of indirect instruments of monetary policy.

- Strengthen and integrate money markets, including the infrastructure. Control by the central bank over the supply of reserve money is the fulcrum of indirect monetary control. Thus, a smoothly functioning market—usually the interbank market—for short-term bank liquidity (central bank money) that can signal and transmit the central bank's actions to all market participants is essential for market-based monetary policy instruments. A prerequisite for smoothly functioning money markets is the availability of a reliable payments, clearing, and settlement system.

- Restructure the banking system and foster competition. For the rapid and transparent transmission of monetary policy actions, it is necessary that the banking sector—and the financial sector in general—be sound and competitive. If commercial banks are not able to respond to monetary policy signals by altering interest rates or liquidity conditions, those signals will not have the desired effects. A bank's ability to respond may be impaired by such factors as management that is not used to a commercial environment, the absence of a hard budget or liquidity constraint, or a financial position so bad that the bank is unable to respond or can respond only in a perverse way. Fostering competition and liberalizing interest rates, therefore, inevitably go hand in hand.

- Adapt the supervisory and regulatory framework to market conditions. Stimulating competition among banks and liberalizing interest rates presuppose the presence of an effective supervisory and regulatory framework to foster prudential behavior by financial institutions. A set of prudential ratios, norms for financial reporting, and disclosure standards are essential elements of such a framework.

- Bolster the technical capacity of the central bank. A minimum requirement for a central bank using indirect instruments of monetary policy is a capacity to project demand for, and supply of, reserves and their impact on broader credit and monetary aggregates. Without this capacity, the central bank will not be in a position to decide on the volume and timing of its interventions. The central bank should also have the legal capacity to use the widest range of indirect instruments of monetary policy to preserve its flexibility.

Directions for the Future

As this overview makes clear, completion of the transition to a market-based financial system in China requires actions along the following lines. As is indicated in Box 1, most of these areas have been explicitly or implicitly recognized by the decision of the Third Plenum.

Institution Building

The newly enacted laws on the People's Bank of China (PBC) and the commercial banks provide the proper legal framework for embarking upon the "commercialization" of the banking system and supporting orderly financial development. The description in Section III has revealed that a major overhaul of the structure and administrative organization of the four state-owned banks is needed. These banks are still largely based on the former command economy system, with a branch structure and hierarchy organized along political-administrative lines. The branches' high degree of independence from headquarters makes liquidity management at a bankwide level difficult and impedes the deployment of indirect instruments by the PBC. The accounting system is also still based on command economy principles, and renminbi and foreign currency accounting is separated in the state-owned specialized banks.

The PBC's task in capacity building lies more in the area of bank supervision than of monetary policy. Work in the latter area will have to concentrate on formulating monetary policy and preparing the infrastructure for the conduct of open market operations. The PBC should be a driving force in implementing the other reform measures discussed below to create the appropriate environment for the use of indirect instruments of monetary policy, that is, an interbank market, liberalized interest rates, and a payments system. Bank supervision that fulfills the requirements of a market system is still in its infancy.

The payments system is still largely cash driven, and the clearing and settlement functions are not yet up to the standards and requirements of more sophisticated financial markets, instruments, and transactions. However, a large project was launched in the early 1990s that will result in the establishment of China's National Automated Payments System (CNAPS), a state-of-the-art payments, clearing, and settlement system, by the end of the decade.

Markets and Instruments

Financial market development has been quite different from that of many other countries. China has fledgling capital markets that provide a solid starting point for the development of more mature markets. The most urgent task lies in developing money markets, that is, markets for short-term funds. Well-functioning, nationally integrated money markets would not only enhance the effectiveness of indirect instruments of monetary policy but also support the capital markets in providing liquidity or funding, or both, for bond portfolios through either loans or repurchase agreements. Money market development has to go hand in hand with institutional and organizational reforms in the banking system, and with improvements in the payments system.

Capital market development has been significant, even though the market and its operations show marked contrasts. While the trade volume has been growing dramatically and the market infrastructure boasts sophisticated, well-functioning electronic trading and matching facilities, the markets are not totally integrated at the national level, which results in persistent price differentials and liquidity shortages. The most important market segment, the government securities market, suffers from the absence of short-term paper. Short-term securities, mainly traded by wholesale agents, would contribute to money market development and the introduction of market-based methods of monetary policy.

It is important for the development of the foreign exchange market to ensure equal access to the market for domestic and foreign banks and enter-

prises, to modernize accounting standards, and to further improve supervision and prudential regulations.

Inherently related to all aspects of market development is interest rate liberalization. The weak financial position of many SOEs and the prospects of insolvency for an increasing number of them has presented a major obstacle to the liberalization of interest rates; however, differences in perceptions among the authorities on the sequencing and the risks of a liberalization of interest rates have also played a major part in slowing down the pace of interest rate liberalization. Consequently, competition in the banking sector, although increasing, is still limited. While there is some nonprice competition, competitive behavior remains constrained by the institutional structure, formal and informal rules and regulations (such as the limited choice of banking for several customers), and the credit plan and its accompanying quota. As is shown by the experience of several other countries, interest rate liberalization will stimulate the development of new financial instruments and thus the diversification of money and capital markets.

The subsequent subsections review in more detail the steps needed to complete the transition to a market-based financial system. These steps relate to interest rate liberalization, the shift to indirect instruments of monetary policy, and the reform of the foreign exchange system.

Interest Rate Liberalization

The liberalization of interest rates in China is undoubtedly a critical—and probably the most difficult—aspect of financial reform. The Third Plenum has set interest rate liberalization by the year 2000 as one of the key actions, and it has become generally recognized that interest rate liberalization should be expedited. The main reasons for liberalizing interest rates are discussed in the next subsection. The following subsection reflects upon some structural impediments to a fast liberalization, and the final subsection presents current thinking in China on the liberalization process.

Reasons for Liberalizing Interest Rates

The main justification for expediting the liberalization of interest rates is the need for a more efficient allocation of financial resources in the Chinese economy. Even though interest rates have remained close to market-clearing levels, it is now generally recognized that liberalization of the interest rates will contribute to more efficient resource allocation in a full-fledged market system.[62] Other reasons relate to the operation of indirect monetary policy instruments, the liberalization of the foreign exchange system, and the growing inconsistencies between the present rate structure and setting and the other reforms in the financial sector.

The effectiveness of indirect instruments of monetary policy greatly depends on the central bank's ability to influence the commercial banks' market behavior and thus their setting of prices. In other words, to the extent that indirect instruments are to become the dominant force in China's monetary policy, interest rates need to be liberalized or at least given greater flexibility.

The opening of the Chinese economy to the rest of the world and the liberalization of the foreign exchange system in 1994 broke the fence that partially shielded domestic financial markets in China from outside markets. This liberalization makes domestic interest rate flexibility not only desirable but also necessary to support the exchange rate and to achieve domestic policy goals, such as combating inflation.

Also, interest rate administration in China is becoming increasingly cumbersome as a result of the rapid changes in the financial system. First, administering the large number of different interest rates set directly by the authorities and trying to maintain their parities are very difficult and cumbersome tasks. Second, under the present rate structure, banks are facing very narrow margins between lending and deposit rates; this will certainly pose problems in the future, when banks will have to make more provisions for loan losses and competition in the market becomes fiercer. Third, the present interest rate structure gives little incentive for the commercial banks to try to raise funds by increasing the deposit base. By financing their credit operations for one year or more through the PBC, banks earn a larger spread and incur lower overhead costs than by using deposits. In such circumstances, the constant pressure on the PBC to extend credit to the commercial banks limits the PBC's freedom to use its lending as a policy instrument.

Finally, the current dual system of interest rate setting—the coexistence of fixed interest rates to be used by the state banks and freer interest rate setting available to other financial institutions—is a source of distortions.[63] The dual interest rate system, besides making arbitrages possible that can fuel speculative activities, results in a segmentation of the money market that will delay the contribution of interest rates to improving the allocative efficiency of financial resources.

Structural Impediments

SOE Impediments

For the liberalization of interest rates to be successful, other countries' experiences suggest that the main economic players (enterprises and financial institutions) should be subject to hard budget constraints to avoid adverse selection problems. Without such constraints, credit could be directed to the most risky borrowers and projects. The recognition of these risks turns the reform of the SOEs into a crucial issue.[64] Many SOEs are operating with extremely narrow profit margins or are incurring losses.[65] Any significant increase in interest rates would rapidly erode those margins and make more enterprises unprofitable. Thus, there is the risk that, if interest rate liberalization is not accompanied by reform of the SOEs, more enterprises will become loss making.

Moreover, interest rate liberalization might fail because of the inverse reaction of insolvent and nonprofit firms to the higher rates that would follow from the liberalization process. Indeed, for SOEs with soft budget constraints, the availability of credit is more important than its cost. Such SOEs would not necessarily be deterred from borrowing at a higher cost; they would simply continue, if they could, to borrow whatever they needed to finance their losses. Some banks might continue lending to such firms, assuming that these loans were ultimately guaranteed by the Government. Raising interest rates in this situation would increase rather than decrease the quantity of credit and, therefore, not produce the desired monetary restraint. The increased demand for credit might drive the interest rates up to such high levels that the cost of borrowing exceeded the expected return on a firm's assets by a significant margin, turn-

---

[62]In general, and compared with many other countries that embarked on broad-based financial reform processes starting from high degrees of financial repression, China's interest rate policy record has been encouraging. During most of the period since 1978, interest rates have been positive in real terms. Only during some episodes of high inflation (1988–89 and 1993–94) have real interest rates turned negative (although indexation schemes reduced the adverse impact of inflation on savings). Even in those periods, the discrepancy, as measured by international standards, was not dramatic. During periods of low inflation, administered interest rates must have been close to market equilibrium level. The favorable assessment of China's overall record on interest rate policy is also supported by the country's continuously high savings ratio. Distortions usually introduced through interest rates that are administratively set below their competitive free market equilibrium level have been less significant than in several other countries.

---

[63]However, the proportion of market interest rates remains small, as evidenced by the large share of credit extended by the state banks (some 80 percent).

[64]It is estimated that the SOE sector still accounts for about 45 percent of industrial production and one third of GNP.

[65]An estimated one third of SOEs are incurring operating losses—accounting for about 6 percent of GNP—that are covered by direct budgetary subsidies and bank lending.

ing solvent, profit-making firms into insolvent ones. Interest rate liberalization might thus have the opposite of the intended effect: it might keep the insolvent borrowers in the market and push the solvent borrowers out of the market.

Reforming the SOEs also involves reforming large parts of the economic and social system. In order to ensure that enterprises are subjected to the discipline of the market, the heavy social burden imposed on them must be addressed, including the provision of employment, social security, and such services as housing and education.

Banking System Impediments

Banking system reform is closely related to SOE reform.[66] Sustained monetary equilibrium requires not only an efficient mix of macroeconomic policies geared toward price stability but also a sound and competitive financial sector whose behavior can be influenced by interest rates signals. There is growing evidence that uncompetitive banking systems and inadequate regulatory frameworks weaken the efficiency of credit allocation, distort the structure of interest rates, and disrupt the transmission of monetary policy signals, with adverse consequences for macroeconomic stabilization.

Progress has been slow in the commercialization of the state-owned commercial banks. These banks continue to face serious structural problems, including significant portfolios of nonperforming loans extended to the SOEs. In the coming years, much progress in commercializing the four state commercial banks is to be expected from the separation of policy and commercial lending, the transfer of the existing stock of policy loans in the portfolios of the state commercial banks to the policy lending banks, the implementation of autonomous financing schemes for the policy lending banks, and the reform of the banks' accounting and tax system.[67] Competition in the banking sector will also improve with the growth of the NBFI sector. The separation of banking and security business activities—which will require the divestment of many NBFIs by the state commercial banks—and the possibility of allowing foreign banks to engage in domestic currency operations on an experimental basis will also stimulate competition.

The enhancement of PBC prudential supervision—a necessary complement to interest rate liberaliza-

tion—will help strengthen the commercialization of banks. Initial steps already undertaken include the generalization of guidelines on asset-liability management and the requirement that banks meet capital adequacy requirements in line with the Basle standards.[68] In addition, the adoption of a loan classification system to identify nonperforming loans and a prescribed gradual increase in provisions for loan losses will facilitate the assessment of the portfolio quality of banks at a later stage.[69] All these reforms will most likely introduce or strengthen the emphasis on profitability in the banking sector and, hence, change the banks' behavior toward interest rate signals.

Forces for Divergence Among Regions

Another legitimate concern regarding interest rate liberalization is its impact on the regions in China (see also Box 9). In a market-based financial system, the allocation of funds has a more anonymous character than in a planned economy. As the "market" sectors grow, the influence of the authorities on the sectoral and geographic allocation of resources through monetary policy will diminish, compared with a system in which a credit plan dominates. At present, the incomplete integration of the markets in China allows the central bank to intervene in one part of the country without spreading the effects of its intervention across the country. The de facto financial integration that will take place under financial liberalization will make money fully fungible and will bring into effect both converging and diverging forces among regions. Convergence will be supported by the tendency of the funds to flow to low-cost areas, while divergence could take place because funds will tend to flow to regions with higher return rates or because local borrowers in lagging regions do not meet the eligibility standards of the banks. Divergence trends will increase the present gap between rich and poor regions in the country and lead to more social and political tensions. As it is unclear whether converging or diverging forces will have the upper hand, the Chinese authorities prefer to liberalize interest rates gradually, as that approach will enable them to correct along the way any major increase in the existing divergences.

Plans for Interest Rate Liberalization

The decision of the Third Plenum called for a reform of interest rate policies and vested the power to formulate interest rate policy in the PBC under the

---

[66]The SOEs are estimated to absorb over 80 percent of total bank credit to the economy.

[67]Policy lending banks are intended to receive capital from the Government, budgetary appropriations, and bond issues. So far, the bulk of the resources have been raised from bond issues, which were allocated to the four state commercial banks according to their share in total deposits, and from PBC lending (in the case of agricultural procurement loans).

[68]According to the authorities, the state commercial banks currently satisfy the "core" capital ratio of 4 percent but fall short of the "second-tier" capital ratio requirement of 4 percent.

[69]Provisions for loan losses are to increase from their 1995 annual average level of 0.6 percent of outstanding loans by 0.1 percent a year until reaching 1 percent of the loan portfolio in 1998.

Box 9. Interest Rate Liberalization and Regional Disparities in China

The theory of regional development and disparities has been developed in the context of market economies: What will be the impact of freely moving production factors on the relative development of regions? This body of theory has also been applied to economic integration, more particularly in the context of the European economic integration: How will the removal of barriers to trade and to the movement of persons and capital across national borders affect the relative wealth of countries and regions in Europe?

By analogy, elements of this theory can also be applied to understand some of the mechanisms underlying the transition from a planned economy to a market economy. The transition from plan to market implies the removal of restrictions on trade of goods and services and on the mobility of people and capital. In general, an economy becomes less segmented when moving from plan to market, and the subsequent integration process can be compared with the economic integration of separate national states.

Economic theory can give some guidance regarding the likely effects of integration; however, it cannot give a clear-cut answer with respect to the emergence and disappearance of regional discrepancies in growth and wealth. It remains very much an empirical question as to whether convergence or divergence will have the upper hand in economic developments in any given country or group of integrating regions or countries.

The "convergence school" postulates that free movement of goods and services will equalize factor returns and living standards. However, this theory uses very strong assumptions that are embedded in the neoclassical theory of international trade. The "divergence school" emphasizes those mechanisms in the economy that will work toward greater divergence, rather than convergence. When barriers to trade and movement disappear, the attractiveness of highly industrialized centers for the location of new activities will increase, and, hence, the divergence among regions will increase. Nevertheless, some authors have stressed that, while these divergence factors may play a role, there will also be counteracting factors, such as enterprises' willingness to take advantage of lower costs in backward regions.

One interpretation of recent developments in China would be that the planned economy has tried to overcome, through the planning mechanism, the tendency toward regional divergence that is visible in market economies. The reforms in China were meant to introduce market elements in the economy. This reform process has introduced greater disparities among regions. More particularly, the policy of establishing Special Economic Zones (SEZs) has favored economic development in such areas as the coastal regions to the detriment of other parts of the country. The removal of the barriers imposed on labor mobility has probably increased the polarization.

However, there were also countervailing forces at work. The credit plan and the use of selective and subsidized credits left the authorities with one instrument to counteract some of the polarization trends and to allocate capital in those areas that tended to be lagging.

These countervailing policies kept some of their effectiveness because of the existence of barriers in the financial markets: there was no national interbank market; and interest rates were administratively set, so that capital could not freely move according to expected returns. Nevertheless, it seems clear that the divergence induced by the unleashing of market forces in some regions has been greater than the convergence forces behind the Government's policies.

The move toward a market-based monetary and financial system in China will be the next step in "marke-

direction of the State Council. This power has been confirmed in the 1995 PBC law. The decision also called for the establishment of a market-oriented rate system by the end of the year 2000.

The PBC's program for interest rate liberalization designed in 1995 in response to the decision of the Third Plenum calls for a gradual approach, based on the belief that China is not ready for an immediate, total liberalization of interest rates. According to this program, the liberalization of interest rates needs to be managed with flexibility, taking advantage of progress in the stabilization of the economy and in structural reforms. Cutting down inflation is seen as a prerequisite, as this would also facilitate the solving of structural problems. Lower inflation rates would allow a return to positive real interest rates, a narrowing of the gap between official and unofficial interest rates, more flexibility in setting administered interest rates, and a reduction of the magnitude of interest rate subsidies.

A first measure following the adoption of these principles in 1995 has been to increase flexibility in the conduct of interest rate policy. For instance, rates have been changed more frequently to signal to the markets the adoption of new strategies; the number of preferential rates has been decreased by eliminating some and merging others; the Government has switched to the use of direct subsidies in the agricultural sector; and international standards for calculating loan rates are gradually being adopted.

Liberalization is planned to be accomplished in three stages, with interbank market, lending, and deposit rates liberalized in turn. (The interest rates in the newly established interbank market were liberalized on June 1, 1996.) The rationale behind this sequencing is that the liberalization of the interbank rate is deemed to have the least political and social exposure, and that lending rates have already been partially liberalized. Deposit rates are tizing" the economy. In a market-based financial system, the influence of the authorities on the sectoral and geographical allocation of funds will diminish compared with a situation in which the credit plan is effectively used. For instance, the People's Bank of China (PBC) mopped up liquidity in some parts of the country in 1993 through the sale of PBC bills and made this liquidity available in other parts of the country. In an integrated financial system where indirect monetary instruments prevail, this type of intervention will become impossible or at least ineffective. These visible forces will be replaced by a more anonymous allocation process. The effects of the financial integration that will follow from financial liberalization will be similar to the effects of the integration of the real economy. Convergence will be supported by two factors. First, as noted above, funds will tend to flow to low-cost areas. Second, increased competition in the financial sector will enlarge the availability of credit for local borrowers in lagging areas .

Divergences could increase among regions, however, because funds will tend to flow to regions with the highest return rates or because local borrowers in lagging regions do not meet the eligibility standards of the banks.

The transition from a segmented to an integrated economy in China bears some resemblance to the gradual financial integration in the United States in the first decades of this century and in the European Union at present. In the United States, segmentation disappeared because of improved communications and transportation. In Europe, national markets are being united with the removal of national borders, which were obstacles to free trade in financial services.

Most countries worldwide have introduced policies or mechanisms to reduce internal welfare discrepancies among regions. The European Union, for one, has established from its inception in 1958 several mechanisms to reduce the social and economic discrepancies

among its countries' regions. However, both literature and country experience indicate that in Europe and elsewhere these mechanisms have had only a limited positive impact on regional developments and often have not achieved the intended goals or, even worse, have introduced other distortions. It seems, therefore, important to be very cautious when introducing mechanisms intended to eliminate regional distortions. As part of the strategy under the (current) Ninth Five-Year Plan, it was decided in 1995 that no more SEZs would be allowed. However, more cities in the underdeveloped interior would be opened to foreign investors. This plan recognized the need to narrow income disparities in China.

In light of these considerations, it has become relevant for China to revisit the current regional policies, which tend to favor the more prosperous regions. While such policies were justified in the initial stages of the reform process, they now seem to widen the gap between rich and poor regions, thereby adding to the problems involved in interest rate liberalization.

If needed, other mechanisms has become could also be selected that, based on the experiences of other countries, are not likely to introduce new discrepancies in financial markets or among the regions. Mechanisms and policies used in other countries can be divided into two broad categories: (i) specialized financial institutions, and (ii) automatic fiscal stabilizers. The use of specialized financial institutions to alleviate regional problems has a mixed record. Therefore, the second approach—the use of automatic stabilizers—deserves closer attention from the Chinese authorities. Some countries—particularly federal states, such as the United States and Germany—have introduced budgetary mechanisms that automatically channel funds from richer to less prosperous states or regions according to specific formulas. These automatic stabilizers usually prevent the regional discrepancies from increasing.

scheduled to be liberalized last because it will take longer for the population to become accustomed to a different way of setting these rates, and also because savings mobilization has so far not been a problem in China. The timing of the liberalization of government securities rates (both short term and long term) as part of this plan has not yet been determined.

Different options are being contemplated for liberalizing bank lending rates. One option would be to follow and broaden the approach adopted since the end of the 1980s, that is, to allow institutions to mark up above the benchmark rates set by the PBC. Another option is to liberalize in order of the types of institutions, with NBFIs and urban credit cooperatives liberalized first, followed by other commercial banks and state commercial banks. Opponents argue that this approach would create unfair competition. A third option would be to liberalize the rates in some regions earlier than in others. However, it is argued

that such an approach could provoke undesirable flows between regions and, in fact, reinforce current regional disparities. In order to ensure transparency in the market and to promote fair competition, consideration is also being given to establishing a mechanism to monitor banks' interest rate spreads.[70]

The sequencing proposed by the authorities is in line with the approach adopted by several countries.

---

[70]In Malaysia and Thailand, measures were taken to ensure transparency in the market and thus fair competition. Banks in the two countries are required to post what is referred to as a "minimum reference rate" in Thailand and a "base lending rate" in Malaysia. These reference rates are based, for each bank, on its average cost of funds and indicate the reference lending rate of that bank for prime-quality customers. In Thailand, the minimum reference rate includes four components: the average cost of funds, the operating cost, a tax levied on financial transactions, and a normal profit margin set at 2 percent. See Mehran, Laurens, and Quintyn (1996).

Box 10. Phases in the Formulation of Monetary Policy in Selected Countries

During the past three decades, countries have gone through three phases in their approach to monetary policymaking. The discretionary approach dominated until the late 1960s in the first phase, the "postwar" phase. The second phase, in the 1970s and 1980s, saw an attempt to identify and follow rules. The most recent period has witnessed the third phase, a return to discretionary policymaking.

Because the gold exchange standard prevailed during the postwar period (the *first phase*), the scope for discretionary monetary policy was limited but by no means absent. For the anchor country (the United States), the exchange rate was not much of a constraint on monetary policy, and the obligation to maintain convertibility of the dollar into gold was of notional significance only. Even the other countries in the system had considerable freedom to implement independent monetary policies, given the existence of exchange controls. During this period, most central banks operated their monetary policies through the adjustment of interest rates in response to perceived changes in demand conditions.

The collapse of the fixed exchange rate system triggered the search for a new anchor for monetary policy. This search was expedited by the surge in inflation that followed in the wake of the first oil shock. The finding in the United States and in a wide range of other countries of a stable relationship between changes in money aggregates and changes in nominal income intensified the interest in monetary rules and

supported the formulation of new monetary policy arrangements. Thus, in the *second phase* of monetary policy, the majority of industrial countries began to use monetary targets. In general, targets were set in terms of broad money rather than base money because broad money was the aggregate theoretically related to income. However, for the three years from 1979, the United States targeted base money to reinforce the public perception of a determined anti-inflationary policy.

Monetary Targeting by the Group of Seven Industrial Countries

Country	Target	Year Started
Germany	Central bank money	1975
Canada	M1	1975
United States	M1	1976
France	M2	1977
Japan	M2 + CDs	1978
United Kingdom	M3	1979
Italy	M2	1984

Countries experienced a fall in inflation following the peak of price increases in the early 1980s. However, it is not clear that the pursuit of intermediate policy targets was the only cause of this success. Indeed, most countries missed their monetary targets, and they did

---

The logic behind this sequencing is that the educational process that necessarily has to accompany nterest rate liberalization should be gradually spread from a core group of sophisticated market parties (bankers and the government) to a wider group of less sophisticated participants (enterprises and the general public).

The pace of liberalization (with the year 2000 as the target) should be monitored constantly. While it is true that other conditions need to be fulfilled for successful liberalization (such as SOE reform), too long a transition period may lead to new distortions in the financial system. One major distortion that emerged in several countries that went through long transitions is disintermediation, which often stemmed from an early liberalization of the interest rates in the NBFI sector.

The Shift to Indirect Monetary Policy

The Third Plenum mandated the PBC to adopt a framework of indirect monetary policy instruments

by 2000. Given China's present exchange regime, which is designed to stabilize the exchange rate, the effectiveness of such an indirect framework will depend on the degree of control that the PBC can exert over its claims on the banking sector, such that changes in that balance sheet item can offset the impact on banks' reserves of fluctuations in net foreign assets. The establishment of reserve requirements in the early years of financial reform and the efforts made by the PBC to centralize its credit to the commercial banks support the development of liquidity management through indirect instruments.

The next steps in the process of reforming monetary policy consist of defining a framework of intermediate and operational targets, refining the existing indirect instruments (reserve requirements and PBC lending to the banks), introducing open market operations, and putting these instruments together in a consistent framework. In establishing this indirect instrument framework, building the appropriate infrastructure to use these instruments efficiently and effectively seems to require more effort than designing the instruments.

not always move quickly to come back down to the pre-scribed growth path.

Most recently, in the *third phase*, the Group of Seven industrial countries has downgraded monetary rules since the late 1980s. The United Kingdom dropped broad money targets in 1986 and continued to monitor only base money (M0). Japan reduced the emphasis on monetary aggregates in 1992. Since the end of the ex-periment with base money control in 1982, the United States has been gradually de-emphasizing monetary aggregates. In 1993, Federal Reserve Chairman Greenspan stated that M2 had been downgraded as a re-liable indicator of financial conditions in the economy, and that no single variable had been identified to take its place. France, which shifted from M2 to M3 in 1991, has set only a medium-term objective since 1994. Canada reduced the emphasis on monetary aggregates as early as 1982; from 1982 to 1991, monetary policy was carried out with price stability as the longer-term goal but without intermediate targets, and targets for re-ducing the rate of inflation were officially announced in early 1991.

Developments in Asian countries have followed along the same lines. Indonesia adopted interest rate targeting following the financial reforms in 1983 be-cause of concerns that targeting monetary aggregates could result in undue increases or instability of interest rates, with possible adverse effects on output. By the end of the 1970s, Singapore approximated the textbook model of an open capital market that was fully inte-grated with global markets. The choice of targeting the exchange rate was determined by the openness of the trade account, which suggested that monetary policy would be most effective if the exchange rate were adopted as its intermediate target. In addition, exchange rate policy is used in Singapore to mitigate external in-flationary pressures. In Korea, monetary targeting is still at the core of the monetary policy framework. However, the annual growth target for M2 has been ap-plied and interpreted flexibly in recent years. Within an annual target range, the approach allows for significant deviations from quarterly targets. It is intended to pre-serve the advantages of monetary targeting—namely, its nominal anchor function and the maintenance of credibility—while capturing the benefits of some de-gree of discretion.

The historical record indicates that countries that maintained a fast pace of financial liberalization often experienced large disturbances in their demand-for-money relationships. Countries that went through less far-reaching reforms or were slower to implement re-forms could place continued reliance on these relation-ships, although judgmental departures from monetary targets have also proved increasingly necessary. Most countries' experiences indicate that monetary targeting should try to find a balance between rules and discre-tion. Approaches that were satisfactory need to be re-viewed as the financial system becomes more sophisti-cated and the external sector becomes more open. More generally, the recent downgrading of monetary target-ing in the third phase of monetary policy coincides with a better control of inflation and the globalization of the international financial markets. Both developments seem to indicate that monetary targeting is most appro-priate to fight strong inflationary pressures in the fast-disappearing closed economy model.

The Target-Instrument Framework

M2 as Intermediate Target

In 1994–95, the PBC made substantial progress in defining a monetary policy framework. While the authorities pursued an exchange rate objective (the stability of the renminbi against the U.S. dollar), they also defined an intermediate target in terms of broad money—M2. Empirical studies suggest that the demand for the three major aggregates in China—currency, narrow money, and broad money—underwent a structural change in 1988, owing to the introduction of a secondary market in government securities and of new financial assets at more market-determined interest rates (Tseng and others (1994)). However, because of the relatively stable long-run demand functions for the monetary aggregates in the post-1988 period, these studies also suggest that monetary targeting can be a feasi-ble exercise. Demand for M2 seems to be more sta-ble than demand for any other aggregate. Further re-search is still needed in this area, particularly because ongoing financial reform and innovation may alter the relationships between the respective monetary aggregates and their right-hand variables, such as real GDP, inflation, and interest rates. Box 10 provides an overview of recent approaches to monetary policymaking in industrialized and se-lected developing countries. The overview indicates that the role of intermediate monetary targets has been downplayed since the late 1980s.

Interest Rates as Operational Target

The selection of an operational target has not been debated much thus far in China, mainly because full reliance on an indirect instrument framework is not expected for some time yet. The choice for most countries is usually between a quantitative variable, such as the central bank's net domestic assets or base money, or an interest rate. Preference for a quantita-tive target is often justified on the grounds that bringing high inflation under control is the central bank's main objective, or that financial markets are not yet sufficiently developed to rely solely on interest rate signals. The main disadvantage of using a quantitative operational target is that its pursuance may induce some undesirable interest rate fluctuations.

Most industrialized countries—which have sophisticated financial markets—rely on short-term interest rates as their operational targets. As is explained in Box 11, two stylized models encompassing a broad spectrum of variants can be adopted. At one extreme, the central bank stays close to the market and intervenes frequently. At the other, the central bank tends to keep a distance from the market by letting it stabilize itself.

As interest rates are liberalized and financial markets develop, the PBC will have to design a framework following one of these two models—or any variant of them—and redesign its instrument framework accordingly. The design of the framework should be based on the PBC's market philosophy (which emphasizes intense involvement versus maintaining a distance), but the choices will be limited in the initial years and determined more by the availability of timely and comprehensive statistics. A more distant approach might thus be necessary in the near future.

Monetary Policy Instruments

Most likely, the PBC's future policy framework will consist of open market operations as the central instrument, supported by reserve requirements and central bank lending or standing facilities. Several technical issues will need to be discussed, such as the relative importance of these various instruments and the proper design of each of them, so that they together form a consistent framework allowing the PBC to absorb and inject liquidity in the financial system in a flexible way. Designing a consistent framework will also facilitate a break with the recent past, in which, as detailed in Section III, the PBC was forced to resort to a multitude of instruments (including PBC financing bills, the recall of loans from banks, and special deposits) to achieve its goals of containing inflation and restoring order in the markets.

The following discussion concentrates on reserve requirements and standing facilities (PBC lending to banks); the conduct of open market operations basically depends on the availability of an adequate microstructure for such operations and is therefore dealt with in the subsequent subsections.

Reform of *reserve requirements* could include the unification of the present two-tier system, once the payments system is working more efficiently, as well as the introduction of averaging procedures. A precondition for easy monitoring of reserve requirements is their aggregation at a bankwide level, instead of the current procedures, in which each bank branch holds its required reserves at the PBC branch at the same administrative level.

For two reasons, *PBC lending to banks* will remain an important monetary policy instrument, at least in the medium term. First, the banking system as a whole—largely because of the financial position of the state commercial banks—shows a structural dependence on PBC credit, a situation that needs time to be reversed.[71] Second, among the range of monetary instruments readily available, PBC credit to banks is potentially the most flexible, particularly because open market operations will, at least in the near future, be too limited in scope to be relied upon solely for liquidity management. Thus, PBC lending facilities should be the main device to inject planned amounts of liquidity into the system.

To enhance the effectiveness of this instrument, it will be necessary in general to move from automatic lending to lending at the PBC's discretion, in line with its monetary program. This shift entails moving from prefinancing arrangements toward refinancing mechanisms. Although the design of new mechanisms for PBC lending has not yet been completed, it appears that—in the context of the overall framework for monetary policy instruments—such a design could be along the following lines.[72]

The first instrument could be a refinance window, through which the PBC provides liquidity on a regular basis to fill the present structural gap of bank resources. The centralization in 1994 of the bulk of PBC credit at the level of the head office was a first step in this direction. Credit could be auctioned in a system in which the PBC sets either the volume (and lets the market decide on the interest rate) or the interest rate, depending on the objectives that it has in mind.

In using this refinance window, two principles should be followed. First, the volume of PBC lending should be determined on the basis of prevailing monetary conditions as derived from a monetary programming framework, with the aim of preventing the formation of excess reserves.[73] Second, the duration of this facility should be short (one week, for in-

---

[71]At the end of September 1994, the PBC's claims on the banking system amounted to ¥952.8 billion and exceeded the banks' required and other deposits at the PBC, which stood at ¥590 billion.

[72]In general, country experiences with refinance instruments indicate that the choice between instruments to provide liquidity to the system as a whole, either through a discretionary and competitive mechanism—at the initiative of the central bank—or through instruments that work on a bilateral basis and at the discretion of the commercial banks—such as a discount window—is to a large extent dictated by the degree of development and liquidity of the money markets, especially the interbank market.

[73]The development of a framework to manage the supply and demand for reserve money at the level of the central bank's balance sheet, that is, a reserve money program, is discussed in the next subsection.

**Box 11. Monetary Policy Framework Models That Focus on
Interest Rates as the Operational Target**

Industrialized countries that fully rely on indirect instruments use basically two stylized models of monetary policy frameworks, with a broad spectrum of variants encompassing these two extremes. The choice of a model depends on the philosophy that the central bank wants to adhere to in its relations with the markets, the stage of development of the financial markets, the technological infrastructure in the markets, and the availability of a timely statistical base.

In one model, the central bank tries to peg the money market rate(s) very narrowly through its open market operations. To achieve this goal, the central bank has to intervene frequently in the market throughout the day. Other instruments, such as required reserves, may be used in this model, but they do not play an active role. The central bank may also have a discount facility at its disposal, but the monetary policy role of this instrument is limited. In this "interventionist" model, open market operations fulfill several goals: they provide and withdraw liquidity, and they are used to steer money market rates and signal changes in the monetary policy stance. This model of permanent presence in the market (which is very much like the U.K. and U.S. models) requires timely statistical information about the markets and highly developed financial markets.

The other extreme is a model wherein the central bank keeps a distance from the market and lets the market to a large extent stabilize itself within the boundaries set by the central bank. In this model, central banks set an interest rate corridor within which market rates can fluctuate, generally by introducing a Lombard facility (at the top of the corridor) and a deposit or discount facility (at the bottom of the corridor). Changes in the two interest rates related to these central bank facilities have a signaling function for the market (as they indicate a change in the stance of monetary policy). Within the corridor, the central bank resorts to open market operations to steer market rates, if deemed necessary.

---

stance) to enhance the flexibility of the PBC's interventions. For this lending window to operate effectively, it has to be supported by a liquid and integrated interbank market, so that liquidity can flow effectively between banks and regions.

This instrument could be supplemented by a type of Lombard facility that would help (branches of) financial institutions settle their end-of-day positions on the books of the PBC. As banks are not yet managing their liquidity on a centralized basis, there might be a need to decentralize this instrument temporarily. The rediscount facility currently operated by the PBC branches under the supervision of PBC headquarters could, with a few transformations, perform the functions of this instrument.

The Supporting Infrastructure

Since the Third Plenum decision in 1993, the PBC has been working steadily to develop supporting measures for open market operations, including a monetary forecasting framework, an integrated interbank market, and clearing and settlement arrangements in support of open market operations.

Liquidity Forecasting Framework

Success in achieving monetary and inflation objectives within a framework of indirect monetary policy depends in part on the PBC's ability to forecast money demand in particular and liquidity developments in general. A reliable forecast for money demand will allow the PBC to set a domestic credit target consistent with the inflation objective. Because China is in the middle of a comprehensive financial sector reform, estimating money demand for forecasting purposes and the related design of a monetary program might be a difficult exercise.

The PBC has recently embarked upon a comprehensive program to identify a money demand function that can be used for policy purposes, as well as functions to forecast inflation, net foreign assets, and other net assets. These estimates will lay the foundation for a liquidity forecasting program that will enable the PBC to plan its monetary policy interventions in the emerging environment. Mainly because several of the required statistics were not available or needed under the planned economy, it will be necessary in this effort to overcome several deficiencies in the statistical apparatus.

An Integrated National Renminbi Interbank Market

In line with the mandate given by the Third Plenum, the PBC started preparing in 1995 for the establishment of an integrated national renminbi interbank market that would supersede the present infrastructure. This work reflects the growing recognition of the importance of an interbank market for the conduct of indirect monetary policy and for money market development in general (Box 12). In light of developments in 1988–89 and again in 1993,

---

Box 12. Interbank Market and Financial Reforms

At the initial stage of financial reform, the establishment of a domestic interbank market is crucial. Such a market is required whether the central bank uses outright open market operations or refinance instruments. Indirect instruments of monetary management operate through changes in the volume of reserves of banks, with which they can settle transactions between themselves (interbank transactions) on the books of the central bank. The decision to change this volume must necessarily rest on the knowledge of the banking system's needs for "settlement funds," and changes in the price for such funds (the interbank market rate) will have an impact on other money market interest rates. Bank reserves can be affected through changes in central bank credit to the banks or through open market operations. Hence, the interbank market plays a major role in transmitting the central bank's policy actions into changes in the behavior of commercial banks, lenders, and borrowers. These behavior changes, in turn, will affect the growth of the monetary aggregates and, more important, the pace of economic activity.

The central bank also has to play an active role in market development. The introduction of indirect instruments at an early stage—even if they cannot be fully effective—can be essential to developing financial markets in general and the interbank market in particular.

The importance of a nationally integrated interbank market for the efficiency and effectiveness of indirect monetary policy has recently been recognized in China. The reform of the interbank market raises four main issues concerning (i) the involvement of the central bank, (ii) the participants in the market, (iii) the degree of centralization of the market, and (iv) the role of the interbank market in the conduct of monetary policy.

With respect to the *involvement of the central bank*, a common feature in many countries embarking on financial reform is the development of the interbank market as a stage-by-stage process, which requires the central bank to take the initiative to promote interbank trading. In Turkey,[1] owing to a variety of factors, some more political than economic, the banking system was highly segmented. Public sector banks were reluctant to lend to private banks not only because of an assessment of commercial risk but also, and perhaps more important, because of political considerations. Similarly, private banks tended to minimize their transactions with other commercial banks owing to competition. In particular, many of the private commercial banks in Turkey belong to different industrial groups. Competition and rivalry among these industrial groups often led to a reluctance on the part of their banks to deal with each other directly and, in particular, discouraged almost completely lending between banks. As a result, an interbank market did not exist in Turkey. However, banks were willing to lend to other banks if their counterpart was the central bank. This situation prompted the central bank to act as a blind broker (the counterpart of all transactions). In order to cover the credit risk, all transactions intermediated by the central bank had to be backed by acceptable collateral, such as government securities.

In Thailand, a repurchase market within the central bank was created in 1979 to further develop the fledgling money market and provide the central bank with a mechanism to monitor and, if necessary, intervene in the market. Participants are allowed to place buying and selling orders with the central bank, indicating the amount, interest rate, and maturity of the desired transactions. The central bank then tries to match the orders and determine a single "market" repurchase rate, that is, a fixing. If needed, the central bank intervenes to absorb or inject liquidity.

In Italy, although an over-the-counter interbank market had been operating for a long time, the central bank was prompted to take action because oligopolistic behavior led to segmentation of the market, and the related excessive volatility impeded the use of interest rates as a channel to transmit monetary policy. In 1990, the central bank promoted the establishment of a screen-based interbank market, accompanied by a thorough modernization of the

---

[1]References to other countries are based on discussions held in a seminar on Interest Rate Liberalization and Money Market Development, jointly sponsored by the Monetary and Exchange Affairs Department of the International Monetary Fund and the

People's Bank of China (PBC), and held in Beijing during July 31–August 9, 1995. The experiences of Korea, Malaysia, Thailand, Turkey, Italy, and the United States were presented and discussed in light of the tentative plans prepared by the PBC. See also Mehran, Laurens, and Quintyn (1996).

---

when the interbank market helped to fuel speculative financing, the authorities considered that the establishment of this market infrastructure and the liberalization of the interbank rate should be accompanied by measures to create order in and standardize the operations of the interbank market. The PBC's intention is to restore orderly conditions, so that the interbank market does not function again as a channel for speculative financing but instead contributes to the development of a broader money market in China and to the transmission of monetary policy. Enhanced efficiency, transparency, and self-discipline are the main goals of the project.

As implemented (on January 1, 1996), the interbank market consists of two levels. The first level—the National Interbank Trading Center—links the headquarters of the commercial banks and 35 Regional Financing Centers (RFCs). The National Inpayments system, enabling a real-time, direct movement of funds on banks' centralized accounts with the central bank. Participation in the system is on a voluntary basis, and participants agree to abide by a set of clear and binding procedures. All interbank transactions among participants on contracts quoted in the system are carried out on the screen-based market and are cleared through the clearinghouse or by entries in the centralized accounts with the central bank. Transactions outside the system are allowed, and nonparticipant banks can freely trade among themselves in all types of deposits on the over-the-counter interbank market.

The involvement of the People's Bank of China in the interbank market is seen in China as a means to restore orderly conditions so that the interbank market does not function as a channel for speculative financing, as occurred in 1988–89 and again in 1993, but instead contributes to the development of a broader money market and to the transmission of monetary policy.

Concerning the *participants in the market*, it should first be noted that a money market is a market that provides economic entities, such as financial institutions, business firms, the government, and individuals, with various kinds of instruments to intermediate their short-term demand for, and supply of, funds. The money market typically includes a repurchase market, secondary markets for securities (treasury bills, commercial paper, and negotiable certificates of deposit), and the interbank market (or call market). As such, the interbank market is the segment of the money market in which financial institutions can trade their deposits held at the central bank. As a consequence, participation in the interbank market is generally confined to financial institutions with current accounts at the central bank. Therefore, interbank markets may or may not include nonbank financial institutions (NBFIs), depending on whether they are authorized to maintain current accounts with the central bank. Only Korea (among the countries discussed here) offers the case of participation by NBFIs, although they are not allowed to maintain settlement accounts with the Bank of Korea.

With respect to the *degree of centralization of the interbank market*, direct transactions between participants in the interbank markets are allowed in all the countries under review. In Turkey, the establishment of an "official" interbank market intermediated by the central bank does not preclude direct transactions between banks. Moreover, the establishment of the official market was seen only as a temporary arrangement to educate partici-

pants and thus facilitate direct transactions. The centralized market structure in Italy is on a voluntary basis. Although it was established under the leadership of the central bank, it operates outside the central bank, which provides only settlement arrangements in support of market transactions. In Thailand, the repurchase market operated by the central bank does not preclude direct transactions between participants. In Korea, participants have the freedom to trade either through a broker system or directly. In Malaysia, the interbank market is an over-the-counter market in which participants are free to trade between themselves, with interbank brokers playing an active role.

With respect to *the role of interbank markets in the conduct of monetary policy*, central banks often deem it appropriate to be directly involved in the development of interbank markets because it is in that segment of the money market that monetary operations, such as credit auctions or repurchase agreements, are likely to take place. Moreover, the interbank market rate is often used as an operational target or a main indicator for the central bank (the federal funds rate in the United States, for instance). As such, the interbank market is the natural playground of central banks. The involvement of the central bank in interbank market development has increased with the shift to indirect instruments of monetary policy and, more particularly, to open market operations.

However, specific operating procedures differ among central banks, according to the stage of development of the various segments of the money market. In the United States, open market operations are conducted in the secondary market for government securities, while the federal funds rate is the operating target. In Thailand, the central bank operates a fixing mechanism for its repurchase window, whereas in other countries the central bank conducts direct bilateral transactions with market participants at the prevailing conditions. Except for the United States and Italy, where open market operations are conducted in the secondary market for government securities, such operations tend to be conducted primarily in the interbank market because that segment of the money market has the highest degree of liquidity.

The desire to develop liquidity management also induced changes in the way that the required reserve ratio operates. In Thailand, Turkey, and Italy, the central bank shifted to an averaging of daily balances in measuring the compliance, in order to limit the volatility of interest rates.

terbank Trading Center is an electronic system that provides market information and a framework for trading. The second level is the 35 RFCs located in 35 provinces, autonomous regions, and cities with independent planning status, as well as the subcenters of the RFCs. These centers and subcenters link the branches of banks at the various administrative levels. Some of these centers have taken a shareholding form; others are organized according to a

membership model; and, in limited cases, the PBC acts as an RFC.

Trading at the first level is done directly between the participants, which are allowed to select their counterparts independently and agree on interest rates for the transactions. Settlement is done directly between the parties through their accounts at the PBC. At the second level, the RFCs are parties to each transaction. However, they are not allowed to maintain open positions at the end of the day, that is, all borrowing from participants must be on-lent before the close of business. As a consequence, the RFCs may be exposed to liquidity and interest risks. Direct transactions between banks outside the financing centers are not permitted. However, the RFCs can operate as brokers between lenders and borrowers. Currently, most transactions at both levels of the market are unsecured.

Participation in the interbank market is open to those financial institutions that have accounts at the PBC—commercial banks and some NBFIs. Lending by NBFIs is not subject to specific limitations; however, such lending is still subject to the limits on volumes and maximum maturity imposed in 1993. Transactions by commercial banks or their branches are also subject to prudential limitations, expressed as a percentage of their deposit base. Institutions not in compliance with the reserve requirement ratio are not allowed to participate.

Daily information on the rates and amount of transactions at the first level is used to calculate the China interbank offered rate (CHIBOR), which is a weighted-average interest rate of all transactions at each maturity—7, 20, 30, 60, 90, and 120 days. The administrative ceiling on interest rates was lifted on June 1, 1996 for interbank transactions at the first level. The CHIBOR serves also as a basis for transactions at the second level.

The rather formal approach adopted by the PBC in creating an interbank market, as opposed to a more informal arrangement allowing for more initiative to be taken by the market participants, is motivated mainly by the PBC's concern that the interbank market may become a permanent source of long-term finance for a number of market participants. While such regulations might be useful in the transitional years, monetary policy should be used to absorb excess liquidity in the system once indirect instruments become fully effective. These absorption operations should prevent funds from flowing out of banks into speculative purposes.

The inclusion of some NBFIs and provincial branches of state commercial banks in the interbank market reflects China's realities today, but it can also be considered a transitional arrangement. Several NBFIs—the trust and investment companies, in particular—collect deposits and perform functions similar to banks. These institutions are also subject to reserve requirements and, by the same token, have accounts at the PBC. In order to monitor their operations more effectively, the authorities intend to impose limits on the maturities and volumes that these institutions can trade in the interbank market. In the same vein, the participation of commercial banks' provincial branches is seen as a necessary transitional arrangement at a time when banks—and espe-

cially the state commercial banks—are still not in a position to conduct centralized liquidity management at the level of the head office.[74]

Nonfinancial institutions have been excluded from the interbank market. Some had been allowed to participate and were in fact often a source of speculative behavior in the market.

A Market Microstructure for Open Market Operations

A number of steps have been taken since 1993 to lay the foundation for the conduct of open market operations using negotiable government securities. In 1993, a system for designating primary dealers was established, and 19 financial institutions were selected. These companies have an obligation to purchase at least 1 percent of each new issue offered by the Ministry of Finance, and they have the privilege of participating in the PBC's future open market operations. However, the initial plan to start some open market operations in 1994 and to rely more heavily on this instrument from 1995 onward (with the elimination of the credit plan) suffered some delay, mainly because of the limited amount of negotiable securities in circulation, the absence of a unified secondary market, and the lack of a proper clearing and settlement infrastructure.

After offering six-month treasury bills on January 25, 1994 and one-year bills on February 1, 1994, the Ministry of Finance did not issue any other bills in that year. It changed its initial intention to roll over treasury bills through frequent sales as the introduction of open market operations was delayed. Also, the resurgence of inflationary pressures in 1994 provoked a shift in the Government's domestic debt-management strategy. The authorities' primary objective became the dampening of inflationary pressures by selling government bonds to individuals to soak up consumer purchasing power. In the second half of 1995, the Ministry of Finance issued ¥ 11.8 billion one-year paperless bonds to primary dealers (¥ 3 billion were sold through an auction). In April 1996, the PBC conducted its first open market operations, using these government securities.

The secondary market in government securities is still small and fragmented (see Section V). Establishment of a nationwide book-entry system within the next few years should alleviate many inefficiencies. However, the enhanced efficiency of the secondary market in government securities will require the establishment of a nationwide market, with all partici-

---

[74]The stipulation in the commercial bank law that a head office has authority over its branches should form the basis for arrangements whereby branches can conduct interbank operations by delegation from headquarters, thus ensuring that the bank's creditworthiness backs each and every transaction at the branch level.

pants in the country having access to the best bids and offers. This achievement, in turn, will require the enhancement of clearing and settlement arrangements.

Clearing and Settlement Arrangements in Support of Open Market Operations

It is expected that China's National Automated Payments System will be up and running by about the turn of the century. Until such time, open market operations will have to rely on the present infrastructure (the Electronic Interbank System) or on interim arrangements. As current clearing and settlement facilities in China are not adequate to support open market operations, the PBC started in 1994 the development of an interim book-entry system for government securities, the Provisional Securities Settlement System, which is intended to be used in the early stages of open market operations. The system is designed to carry government securities, but small modifications would allow it to deal in other types of securities as well (such as financing bonds issued by the newly established policy lending banks). An interesting feature of the system is that it is designed for transactions between PBC headquarters and the headquarters of major banks. This in itself could give a significant impetus to centralized liquidity management, by state commercial banks in particular.

Next Steps in Foreign Exchange Reform

Foreign exchange reform has received a major boost since 1993–94. The following steps could be taken in the near future to establish a genuine foreign exchange interbank market governed by regulations that meet international standards.

Alternatives for Developing Exchange Markets

In developing an exchange market in China with the objective of eventually establishing a regular interbank market, the authorities face two basic alternative routes. Development could continue in the context of the CFETS, or direct dealing between financial institutions could be introduced. While the latter is the stated long-term goal, the CFETS could serve a useful function during the transitional period while institutions are developing needed skills and procedures.

An extension of trading hours would provide the banks with a current basis for setting buying and selling rates in their customer transactions throughout the day. Furthermore, it would increase the gross flows to the CFETS market. Because transactions would be conducted on a continuous basis with the market, there would be fewer possibilities for inter-

nal netting of transactions, and the exchange market would become deeper and more liquid. The adoption of modern risk-management techniques and prudential regulations will eventually force trading at each financial institution to be centralized at its head office or at only one branch.

The system should also eventually allow for direct bilateral settlement and for the possibility of rejecting a counterpart for credit risk reasons. It is important that member institutions assume all the credit risks in the system, although it will take some time for authorized dealers to get used to evaluating the creditworthiness of other market counterparts.

Supervising and Regulating Banks' Foreign Exchange Operations

Issues to be addressed in this area range from reform of the accounting system and the banks' internal structure to the institution of prudential regulations. Introduction of a new accounting system based on international standards is expected in 1997–98. The present separation between accounting in renminbi and accounting in foreign currency would disappear under this new system. The commercial bank law places branches under the authority of their headquarters. These stipulations should be enforced over time to clarify the relationships between branches and headquarters.

In an environment of fluctuating exchange rates and interest rates, responsible banking will have to be based on awareness of, and continuous control over, risks. It is, therefore, important that modern prudential regulations for banks' foreign exchange operations and risks be introduced as soon as possible in China. These regulations and risk limits should replace the current (minimum) limits on banks' liquid foreign assets. Each financial institution should be given only one global limit; if it wishes to, it could internally decide that part of the limit could be utilized by a branch or branches. Within the scope of the flexibility provided by the exposure limits, banks could be allowed to trade foreign exchange for their own accounts at any time.

Financial Institutions' Operational and Managerial Capabilities

Despite the apparent depth and diversity of the financial system, the market is dominated by one bank, the Bank of China (BOC), which represents some 80 percent of exchange market transactions. The BOC is the only truly international institution, with 474 branches in 18 countries and territories. Most other banks have engaged in foreign exchange operations for only a few years, although some are very large institutions in the domestic market. However, the situation is changing rapidly, with all licensed banks rapidly establishing foreign relationships and, in many cases, representative offices, branches, or subsidiaries.

The fact that branches of banks in different provinces also have separate foreign exchange licenses, capital, and dealing functions complicates risk and position management. Although some branches have very limited rights, others are authorized to establish independent positions. Telecommunications and the exchange of information about transactions are apparently not problems for most banks. However, global risk monitoring and management often take place on only a monthly, quarterly, or annual basis. Many bank branches active in foreign exchange operations view themselves as separate banks with their own foreign-currency-denominated balance sheets; they measure their risks in U.S. dollars, not in renminbi. Many institutions may therefore have larger renminbi exposures than prudential banking would warrant.

It will not be long before Chinese banks link their major operations on-line to each other. This process will be expedited if there are competitive pressures on banks to move in this direction. This linkage will make it possible to quote and disseminate current rates throughout the country. When some banks start quoting current competitive exchange rates to major customers, other banks will follow. Transactions between banks and their customers will then typically be priced by banks on the basis of the prevailing market rate.

Market evolution and market making would also be easier if the settlement period for retail transactions were the same as (or longer than) the settlement period (currently one day) in the CFETS market. Otherwise, it will be difficult for banks to cover their retail transactions through purchases and sales in the wholesale market, and they will not be in full control of their foreign exchange positions.

Eventually, banks will also have to assume the credit risk of dealing. This assumption of risk could start through the introduction of direct bilateral settlement between transaction counterparts. Under such arrangements, dealers would have to establish credit limits for all their counterparts.

Forward Operations

There is no forward exchange market in China at this time, although the need for one is obvious. Banks should be in a position to quote forward rates and hedge forward transactions across a broad range of maturities. To do this, banks will need to have access to international foreign exchange and money markets. As discussed above, an embryonic domestic money market is beginning to emerge in China, although interest rates are not yet fully free. Hedging and the pricing of forward transactions should thus now be possible. Forward operations would speed up the integration of banks' foreign exchange and domestic operations.

Leveling the Playing Field and Strengthening the Environment for Competition

Markets are most efficient in allocating and redistributing resources when all market participants are subject to the same rules and regulations. This is not yet the case in China. Foreign funded enterprises (FFEs) have the right to retain foreign exchange while domestic enterprises are subject to a surrender requirement. FFEs also can enter the CFETS directly while domestic enterprises have to deal through financial institutions. Moreover, foreign banks are restricted in their business activities essentially to handling sales of foreign exchange for FFEs. Addressing these issues constructively will help to strengthen the emerging exchange market mechanisms further.

X   Assessment and Conclusions

It is generally accepted that financial sector reform is a complex and highly country-specific undertaking, despite the existence of some general guiding principles regarding its preconditions and sequencing. The length and depth of the process, by definition, depend a great deal on the conditions at the start of the reform. In the unique case of China, financial development had to start from a very low level, for the financial sector was almost nonexistent at the start of the process. Seen against this background, China's record of financial sector building has been impressive, but the agenda for further reform remains highly challenging as well.

During the first 15 years of reform, China's financial sector has been developing on the border of two economic systems: plan and market. Thus, the newly established financial institutions—including the People's Bank of China (PBC)—had to operate in an intermediate control system. The continuing dominance of planning devices in the monetary sector and the authorities' preference to keep the financial sector as the main vehicle for an interventionist economic development strategy are primarily responsible for the failure of the larger financial institutions to evolve into genuine "commercial banks." Smaller banks and nonbank financial institutions (NBFIs) have enjoyed more freedom (they were not subject to the core credit plan and were given more leeway in setting lending rates), but they remained for a long time on the margin of the sector's growth, at least quantitatively.[75]

The upshot of the reform strategy adopted thus far—an emphasis on institution building with only a small dose of financial liberalization—naturally leads to the conclusion that in the agenda for future financial reform the point of gravity will have to lie on liberalization measures, in particular of the interest rates and the exchange system. To be successful, these liberalization measures will need to be under-

pinned by other reforms, such as the establishment of a banking supervision function, reform of the banks' accounting system, and the full separation of policy from commercial lending. In turn, liberalization will give a new impetus to money and capital market development and the concomitant development of new financial instruments. These advances, taken together, will enhance the effectiveness of indirect monetary policy instruments, which will complete China's transition to a market-based financial system and thereby increase the efficiency of resource allocation in the economy.

Whereas China's reforms of the past 15 years have been unique—largely because of the existence of an intermediate control framework—this assessment suggests that in the near future China will find itself on a path that looks familiar to several other countries worldwide, namely, one of financial liberalization. Indeed, the measures listed above are on the agenda of many countries that, following their initial years of institution building, are embarking on financial liberalization programs. For example, many countries in Eastern Europe and the Baltics, as well as Russia and other countries of the former Soviet Union, are still in the liberalization phase, even though they went through a shorter period of institution building and virtually bypassed the phase of intermediate controls.

The following subsection highlights the main characteristics of China's financial sector development. The final subsection reviews the challenges that lie ahead. Both subsections try to point out some lessons for reforms under way in other countries.

Main Characteristics of Financial Sector Development

Diversification of Financial Sector

Starting from a system in which a few "banks" operated as government departments to implement the credit plan—in fact, they played mere accounting roles—the authorities have managed to establish a fairly diversified financial sector, with universal and

---

[75]The characteristic of stimulating small institutions alongside large, state-owned ones is also found in other sectors of China's economy. See, for example, the development of the small and collectively owned township and village enterprises versus that of the large state-owned enterprises.

regional banks and a variety of NBFIs. However, the sector remains dominated by four state-owned banks. These banks lack financial sophistication, owing to the interference of policy-based lending in their management decisions, their internal structures (which give the branches a high degree of independence from their headquarters), and technical factors, such as the lack of modern accounting practices.

Accessibility of Financial Sector

From the early days on, the Government managed to extend the financial system fairly evenly across the vast country, a factor that has certainly added to the country's high savings ratio and its high degree of monetization. At this stage, the country's economic reforms in general benefit from this part of the reform strategy. Making the financial system accessible to the entire country is not easy in a country as large as China and is often neglected in financial reforms in many other smaller countries.

Interplay of Government Plans and Market Forces

In line with the approach adopted by several other Asian countries, the Chinese Government tried during the first 15 years of reform to hold a firm grip on financial market development to ensure that the financial sector—in particular, the four specialized banks and the government securities market—remained a major vehicle for its financial policies. However, in both the banking sector and the capital markets, emerging market forces started to interact with the Government's plans, leading to interesting results. In some cases, market forces reinforced the Government's actions; in other cases, they interfered with those actions. For instance, the Government remained very selective until the early 1990s in allowing new banks to be established; however, a significant NBFI sector started mushrooming naturally in the mid-1980s. This sector has enriched the financial landscape, but it has also posed challenges for the Government, which was forced to include certain types of NBFIs in the credit plan to ensure that proper coverage was continued.

In another area—the government securities market—the market itself initiated secondary market trading, which was afterward officially allowed. This development also posed new challenges for the Government. For instance, the market wanted secondary market price movements to be reflected in the new issues, whereas the Government tried to stick to its administratively set yields and prices. On some occasions, such as in 1993, the Government ultimately had to follow the market and raise the interest rate at issue.

Capital Markets and Money Markets

Capital markets are much more developed than money markets in China. Several factors account for this unusual sequencing. First, the Government had pushed for the issuance of government securities as an alternative means of tapping household savings and complementing financing through the credit plan. Second, banks were not offered many alternatives to invest their "free" resources, particularly during the first years of reforms, and incentives to search for such alternatives were in part undermined by the PBC's practice of paying high interest rates on deposits made at the PBC. Banks also started channeling some surplus funds through their affiliated NBFIs to circumvent the credit quotas. Third, interbank and intrabank markets were not encouraged for a long time because local authorities were not keen on transferring financial surpluses out of their regions. Fourth, the banks' administrative organization and the state of advancement of the payments system were not conducive to the development of nationwide money markets.

These reasons help explain why the interbank market—usually the first segment of a money market to be developed—got off the ground so slowly. In addition, the Government was until recently reluctant to issue short-term securities—typically another pillar of money market development—for administrative and logistical reasons. Capital market development, however, has been quite successful, although the market is still very "retail" in nature, lacks liquidity, and is not fully integrated on a national scale. The lack of liquidity is largely due to the missing money market. In general, the establishment of a money market looms as one of the main challenges in the near future, as it will tie together various currently isolated segments of the Chinese financial markets and give a further impetus to capital market development.

Role of the PBC and Underlying Legal Framework

From the first days of its establishment, the PBC has played a significant role in China's emerging financial system, even though it lacked for a long time the proper legal underpinnings for this job. Until recently, the central bank's objective was ambiguously defined. In the changing system, it was still considered the lender of *first* resort, while, as a central bank, it was trying to evolve into the lender of *last* resort. In the process, these two objectives were bound to collide.

As emerging market forces began to be felt and the financial system expanded, the authorities recognized the need to strengthen the PBC's supervisory authority. Initially, the PBC's relationship with the state-owned banks was only that of *primus inter pares*, but gradually it established its authority over these banks and over the newly emerging parts of the financial system, namely, other banks and NBFIs. In the absence of a legal framework, the PBC has tried to fill the supervisory and regulatory vacuum by supervising the banks and regulating the NBFIs. The PBC was also closely involved in promulgating rules and regulations for securities exchanges and stock markets. However, the country's political and administrative structure and the tendency to decentralize decision making, combined with the lack of supporting legislation, put the PBC in an awkward position in which local authorities had more influence over PBC branches and branches of the specialized banks than did PBC's headquarters. This situation has changed only marginally, but it is expected that the PBC law and the commercial bank law will strengthen the authority of the PBC over the financial sector, as well as the autonomy of the financial sector vis-à-vis local authorities.

More generally, the design of the legal framework underpinning financial transactions in a market-based economy has been taking shape only since 1993. The lack of attention paid to the establishment of a legal framework in support of financial development in the first decade of reform probably also delayed the commercialization of the state-owned banks. Their protracted dependence on the Government and its policies has resulted in their failure to become more sophisticated financially and has prevented them from making more effective use of financial instruments in their operations. In addition, the state-owned banks' internal administrative and managerial structures, which have given branches a high degree of independence from their headquarters, have made it difficult for these banks to operate in a market environment. Technical factors, such as the lack of modern accounting practices, have aggravated these problems.

Transition to Indirect Monetary Policy Instruments

The PBC has also tried to diversify its monetary policy instruments by introducing reserve requirements and lending facilities to banks. Thus far, these modifications have had only limited effects for several reasons. First, the credit plan and related policy-based lending have continued playing a dominant role. Second, the absence of any significant interest rate liberalization has limited these instruments' usefulness. Third, in the absence of money markets, both instruments were in fact used to channel liquidity from one region to another or from one bank to another: mopping up through the reserve requirements and lending back through the PBC's lending facilities. As a result, the PBC's balance sheet has also been inflated.

Interest Rate Liberalization

Interest rates are being liberalized late in the process. For a long time, political resistance against interest rate liberalization was strong, mainly because of the weak financial position of the state-owned enterprises (SOEs). While a simplification of the administrative interest rate structure and more flexibility in setting the rates could have been introduced earlier in the reform process, large-scale liberalization of the rates could only have taken place if other reforms affecting the functioning of the financial sector had been addressed earlier, such as the organization of the state-owned specialized banks and bank accounting. The decision of the Third Plenum dealt with this chicken-and-egg problem directly.

Exchange System

The Chinese authorities have so far proceeded with determination in liberalizing the exchange system and opening the economy. Recent years have witnessed a rapid succession of decisions that have almost invariably been taken earlier than outside observers had expected and much faster than stated in the timetables.

The Chinese exchange system is de facto already very close to current account convertibility. The authorities have indicated that China will accept the obligations under Article VIII of the IMF's Articles of Agreement with respect to current account convertibility before the year 2000. This timetable may well turn out to be a very conservative estimate; with the exchange system already quite open, full convertibility of the renminbi may well come soon after current account convertibility.

At this time, foreign sector liberalization is moving faster than domestic liberalization. Because large capital inflows have supported the balance of payments since 1993–94, there was no pressure on the exchange rate, and the foreign exchange system reforms have proved successful so far. However, difficulties in monitoring liquidity in the system arising from the unavailability of domestic sterilization instruments complicated the PBC's monetary management. In the circumstances, external liberalization might become a driving force for further domestic liberalization, for example, with respect to interest rates.

The Challenges Ahead

The current actions of the authorities to liberalize interest rates and establish a nationally integrated interbank market are at the core of their efforts to establish a liberal and efficient financial system by the end of the century. To be successful, however, these plans need to be complemented by further progress in other areas of financial sector reform.

Commercialization of State Banks and Level Playing Field

Commercialization of the four state banks needs to be expedited. To this end, the policy lending banks should become the only vehicles for noncommercial lending. Reform of the banks' accounting system is another necessity, as is the further development of the legal framework for financial transactions.

Domestic and external liberalization should also go hand in hand with the leveling of the playing field for domestic and foreign banks. With the further opening of the financial system, the current regulatory constraints on foreign banks in relation to domestic banks will have to be addressed. Foreign banks can, through competition and example, contribute to the modernization of the Chinese banking system.

Increasing openness will also place ever greater demands on both commercial banks and authorities. In order to be competitive, Chinese commercial banks will have to integrate foreign operations into their general banking under the planned accounting reforms. Also, great strains will be placed on banks' risk-management functions until the relationship of branches to head offices has been settled: overall risk management must be centralized.

Prudential regulation and bank supervision must cover all aspects of banking in a unified manner, regardless of whether operations take place in China or in a branch abroad, or in local or foreign currency. Effective overall supervision remains difficult in the current decentralized framework. In this connection, there will also be increasing pressure to integrate under one body the supervisory responsibilities that are currently divided between the PBC and the State Administration for Exchange Control (SAEC).

Foreign Exchange Market Development

Foreign exchange trading in the wholesale market can develop along two routes. Trading can continue to be channeled through the China Foreign Exchange Trade System (CFETS), or direct trading between banks may emerge. The CFETS may also continue to have a role, at least for a while, in ensuring uniform access to foreign exchange also for smaller enterprises and outlying regions. In the longer run, as Chinese banking is integrated into the international financial system, standard international trading procedures will be adopted, including direct trading between market participants. The evolution of the direct-dealing market will also help introduce modern risk-management techniques to Chinese banks.

Coordination of Monetary and Exchange Rate Policy

Removing the few remaining constraints on capital movements will further accentuate the need for a strengthening and integration of monetary and foreign exchange operations and their management under one authority. To this end, the SAEC, if it continues to exist as an independent organization, must coordinate its operations on a daily basis with the open market desk that will emerge at the PBC. The ability of the authorities to manage monetary aggregates efficiently will be critical to further stable growth.

Real Sector Reform

The effectiveness of these domestic and external financial sector reforms will depend largely on progress achieved in structural reforms in other sectors of the Chinese economy outside the control of the monetary authorities. In this respect, the reform of the SOEs will be of extreme importance. The PBC will have to take advantage of progress in the reform of the real sector and utilize every opportunity to expedite the process of financial liberalization. An additional and welcome advantage is the strong commitment at the highest political level to move ahead in developing market mechanisms, as evidenced by the enhanced authority given to the PBC in the new central banking law.

Appendix   Chronology of Financial and Exchange System Reforms

The major reforms undertaken in the exchange system, banking sector, money and capital markets, and monetary policy from 1978 to 1995 are presented on pages 86–88. The reforms are grouped chronologically. The first phase (1978–84) marked the re-establishment of the financial and exchange system, and the second phase (1984–88) witnessed its diversification. The third phase (1988–91) was characterized by recentralization of the financial and exchange system, while commercialization and expansion marked the fourth phase (1992–95).

Chronology of Financial and Exchange System Reforms

Phase	Exchange System	Banking Sector	Money and Capital Markets	Monetary Policy
First Phase: Re-establishment of the Banking System (1978–84) **December 1978** Third Plenum of the Central Committee of the Communist Party makes a decisive break with the legacy of the Cultural Revolution and resolves to focus the Party's work on economic development in order to achieve substantial, sustained gains in output. To achieve this objective, it is decided that market-oriented reforms will be adopted.	**1981** A single exchange rate is established for internal settlement of trade transactions. An experimental trading system is established by the BOC in a few cities, where domestic enterprises are permitted to sell foreign exchange to other domestic enterprises at the internal settlement rate. The BOC acts as broker.	**1979** Allocation of investment funds shifts from budgetary grants to bank lending. Three specialized banks are established to operate in specific sectors of the economy (PCBC, BOC, and ABC). A network of RCCs is set up under the supervision of the ABC.	**1981** The issuance of government securities is resumed through compulsory sales to enterprises and individuals.	**1978–84** Monetary policy is still dominated by the credit plan and the cash plan, the financial counterparts of the physical plan. Interest rates are set by the PBC under the authority of the State Council.
		Early 1980s The first NBFIs start to operate, including a number in the coastal regions (ITICs mainly), quite often at the provincial level.	**1982** Private enterprises are allowed to issue shares.	
Second Phase: Diversification and Innovation (1984–88) **September 1983** A directive of the State Council formally establishes the PBC as the country's central bank by removing its urban commercial activities, thereby finalizing the transition to a two-tier banking system.	**1985** The use of the settlement rate is discontinued. All transactions are to be done at the official rate set by the SAEC. **1986** The foreign exchange regime is changed from one of pegging to a basket to a system of managed floating. Chinese enterprises and foreign investment corporations in SEZs are permitted to transact foreign exchange at freely negotiated rates (the retention quota system).	**1985** A fourth specialized bank, the ICBC, is established to take over the commercial activities that were removed from the PBC. **1986** Provisional regulations entrust the PBC with responsibility to conduct monetary policy and regulate and supervise the financial system, as well as the money and capital markets. All banks are allowed to engage in foreign exchange transactions. UCCs are opened under ICBC supervision, and TICs and securities houses proliferate.	**1983** The ABC establishes prototype intrabank market; other banks follow. **1984** The first information centers appear in some major cities, thereby introducing the concept of an interbank market. Local enterprises are allowed to issue corporate bonds with the prior approval of the PBC. Interest rates on these bonds are allowed to be up to 40 percent higher than rates on bank deposits. **1985** SOEs are permitted to issue shares carrying no ownership rights. Banks are permitted, upon approval from PBC, to issue financial bonds. The interest rate is set 2 percentage points above deposit rates of similar maturities.	**1984** Reserve requirements are introduced; different rates apply according to the type of deposits (20–40 percent). PBC establishes lending facilities for banks. **1985** Ratio of reserve requirements is reduced and made uniform at 10 percent. **1986** Banks are allowed to adjust interest rates on loans within a 10 percent margin above the administered rate. Credit quotas become more indicative.

1987

Ratio of reserve requirements is raised to 12 percent.

1987

Two "universal" banks are permitted to compete with existing banks in all forms of business.

1986

Secondary market trading in government securities is allowed on an experimental basis.

1987

The Government begins to diversify its debt instruments with the issuance of key construction bonds, state construction bonds, and special state bonds to households and state enterprises.

1988

Ratio of reserve requirements is raised to 13 percent.

Third Phase: Rectification and Recentralization (1988–91)

Early 1988

In the wake of a bout of inflationary pressures, a stabilization program is introduced (the "rectification program"), in which structural reforms are given lower priority than stabilization and administrative measures are used to supplement nascent indirect instruments of macroeconomic control.

1988

The right to trade in retention quotas is extended to all domestic entities engaged in foreign trade. Those who were also permitted to retain foreign exchange earnings are permitted to transact retention quotas in the swap centers. By October 1988, 80 swap centers have been established.

1988

The State Council officially approves trading in government securities. Gradually, trading is extended from 7 cities to 63 cities, and other securities (bonds, shares, and nongovernment securities) are added to the list. Fiscal bonds are sold for the first time to financial institutions.

1988

The TIC sector is reorganized: the number of TICs is significantly reduced through mergers and absorptions.

1989

Guidelines on "excess reserve requirements" are introduced in a range of 5–7 percent of domestic currency deposits.

The 1986 measure allowing banks to adjust loan rates above the administered rate is reversed. Credit quotas again become mandatory.

1989

The Stock Exchange Executive Council is founded.

1988–89

Official rate is used for the foreign exchange plan, the surrender of foreign exchange, and purchases made with retention quotas.

1989

The SAEC issues regulations on priority access to foreign exchange traded in swap centers.

1990

Banks are again allowed to adjust interest rates on loans within specified margins (60 percent for RCCs, 30 percent for UCCs, and 20 percent for the other banking institutions) above rate set by PBC.

The PBC regulates interbank market rates and promulgates new measures to regulate interbank markets.

1990

High inflation prompts the Government to issue "price-indexed" bonds.

The PBC establishes the Quotation Center for government securities. The Shanghai Securities Exchange is officially recognized.

1991

The Shenzhen Stock Exchange is officially recognized. Treasury bonds for households are issued via an experimental underwriting syndicate.

Chronology of Reforms (concluded)

Phase	Exchange System	Banking Sector	Money and Capital Markets	Monetary Policy
Fourth Phase: Commercialization and Expansion (1992–Present)				
October 1992 Fourteenth National Congress of the Communist Party endorses the views of senior leader Deng Xiaoping and adopts goal of establishing a "socialist market economy."	**1992** Part of the retention quotas made available to the state are purchased at a premium equal to the monthly weighted average of the rate in the swap market. The PBC starts selling the quotas that it has bought at the market rate to importers through the swap market at the prevailing swap market rate.	**1992** The rectification program ends. The authorities announce their intention to accelerate the reform process. Gradually, more commercial banks, mostly of regional scope, are licensed.	**1993** The Quotation Center is transformed into the NETS.	**1993** Banks and NBFIs are ordered to recall all loans on the interbank market granted to finance real estate or securities. The PBC issues new guidelines on interbank activities.
November 1993 Third Plenum of the Fourteenth Central Committee outlines and approves a comprehensive reform strategy in which financial reforms are mentioned as a key element to strengthen the capability for market-oriented macro-economic management.	**1993** The State Council decides that the SAEC should function under the guidance of the PBC. The PBC lifts the cap on the swap rate. The SAEC issues regulations on licensing, capital, operations, controls, and risk limits for foreign exchange operations.	**1994** Three policy lending banks are established.	**1994** Paperless treasury bills are issued through an underwriting syndicate. The PSSS, planned to be the (temporary) infrastructure for payment and settlement related to open market operations, is established.	**1994** Decision is made to extend the bulk of PBC credit at the PBC headquarters level, thereby reversing the previous practice of extending credit at the branch level. PBC overdraft or direct loans to the Government are discontinued. Some PBC loans extended to the state commercial banks and other financial institutions are called back for monetary policy purposes. Special deposits are used to absorb excess liquidity in the system. Guidelines on asset-liability management are introduced for all banks, and credit quotas are replaced by loan-to-deposit ratios for the UCCs and TICs. Only four state commercial banks and four universal banks remain under credit quotas.
	1994 The official and swap market exchange rates are unified at the prevailing swap market exchange rate. The CFETS becomes operational, creating an integrated system of foreign exchange trading centralized in Shanghai.	**1995** The PBC law is enacted. The commercial bank law is enacted.	**1995** Plans are prepared to liberalize interest rates and to develop an integrated interbank market.	**1995** Excess reserve guidelines are complied with on a consolidated, bankwide level, while monitoring remains at the branch level.

Bibliography

Alexander, William, and others, *The Adoption of Indirect Instruments of Monetary Policy*, IMF Occasional Paper 126 (Washington: International Monetary Fund, June 1995).

Bell, Michael, Hoe Ee Khor, and Kalpana Kochhar, *China at the Threshold of a Market Economy*, IMF Occasional Paper 107 (Washington: International Monetary Fund, September 1993).

Blejer, Mario, and others, *China: Economic Reform and Macroeconomic Management*, IMF Occasional Paper 76 (Washington: International Monetary Fund, January 1991).

Dalla, Ismail, *The Emerging Asian Bond Market* (Washington: World Bank, 1995).

De Wulf, Luc, and David Goldsbrough, "The Evolving Role of Monetary Policy in China," *Staff Papers*, International Monetary Fund (Washington), Vol. 33 (June 1986), pp. 209–42.

Fan, Qimiao, and Peter Nolan, eds., *China's Economic Reforms: The Costs and Benefits of Incrementalism* (New York: St. Martin's Press, 1994).

Girardin, Eric, "Difficulties with Credit Control and Financial Sector Reform in China," OECD Development Center Studies (Paris: Organization for Economic Cooperation and Development, June 1995).

Goldstein, Morris, David Folkerts-Landau, and others, *International Capital Markets: Developments, Prospects, and Policy Issues* (Washington: International Monetary Fund, September 1994).

Huang, Guabo, "Problems of Monetary Control in China: Targets, Behavior and Mechanism," in *China's Economic Reforms: The Costs and Benefits of Incrementalism*, ed. by Qimiao Fan and Peter Nolan (New York: St. Martin's Press, 1994).

Khor, Hoe Ee, "China—Macroeconomic Cycles in the 1980s," IMF Working Paper 91/85 (Washington: International Monetary Fund, September 1991).

——, "China's Foreign Currency Swap Market," IMF Paper on Policy Analysis and Assessment 94/1 (Washington: International Monetary Fund, December 1993).

McKinnon, Ronald I., *Financial Growth and Macroeconomic Stability in China, 1978–92: Implications for Russia and Eastern Europe* (Washington: International Monetary Fund, 1993).

Mehran, Hassanali, Bernard Laurens, and Marc Quintyn, "Interest Rate Liberalization and Money Market Development in a Selected Number of Countries" (Washington: International Monetary Fund, forthcoming, 1996).

People's Bank of China (1994a), *Annual Report 1994* (Beijing: People's Bank of China, 1994).

—— (1994b), *China's Financial Outlook 1994* (Beijing: People's Bank of China, 1994).

——, *Annual Report 1995* (Beijing: People's Bank of China, 1995).

——, *Almanac of China's Finance and Banking*, various years.

Perkins, Dwight H., "Reforming China's Economic System," *Journal of Economic Literature*, Vol. 26 (June 1988), pp. 601–45.

Sachs, Jeffrey, and Wing Thye Woo, "Structural Factors in the Economic Reforms of China, Eastern Europe, and the Former Soviet Union," *Economic Policy,* No. 18 (April 1994), pp. 102–43.

Santorum, Anita, "The Control of Money Supply in Developing Countries: China 1949–1988," ODI Working Paper 29 (London: Overseas Development Institute, April 1989).

Tseng, Wanda, and others, *Economic Reform in China: A New Phase*, IMF Occasional Paper 114 (Washington: International Monetary Fund, November 1994).

World Bank, "China Financial Sector Review: Financial Policies and Institutional Development" (unpublished; Washington: World Bank, 1990).

——, *The East Asian Miracle: Economic Growth and Public Policy* (New York: Oxford University Press for the World Bank, 1993).

——, *The Emerging Asian Bond Market—China* (Washington: World Bank, 1995).

Yi, Gang, *Money, Banking, and Financial Markets in China* (Boulder, Colorado: Westview Press, 1994).

Recent Occasional Papers of the International Monetary Fund

141. Monetary and Exchange System Reforms in China: An Experiment in Gradualism, by Hassanali Mehran, Marc Quintyn, Tom Nordman, and Bernard Laurens. 1996.

140. Government Reform in New Zealand, by Graham C. Scott. 1996.

139. Reinvigorating Growth in Developing Countries: Lessons from Adjustment Policies in Eight Economies, by David Goldsbrough, Sharmini Coorey, Louis Dicks-Mireaux, Balazs Horvath, Kalpana Kochhar, Mauro Mecagni, Erik Offerdal, and Jianping Zhou. 1996.

138. Aftermath of the CFA Franc Devaluation, by Jean A.P. Clément, with Johannes Mueller, Stéphane Cossé, and Jean Le Dem. 1996.

137. The Lao People's Democratic Republic: Systemic Transformation and Adjustment, edited by Ichiro Otani and Chi Do Pham. 1996.

136. Jordan: Strategy for Adjustment and Growth, edited by Edouard Maciejewski and Ahsan Mansur. 1996.

135. Vietnam: Transition to a Market Economy, by John R. Dodsworth, Erich Spitäller, Michael Braulke, Keon Hyok Lee, Kenneth Miranda, Christian Mulder, Hisanobu Shishido, and Krishna Srinivasan. 1996.

134. India: Economic Reform and Growth, by Ajai Chopra, Charles Collyns, Richard Hemming, and Karen Parker with Woosik Chu and Oliver Fratzscher. 1995.

133. Policy Experiences and Issues in the Baltics, Russia, and Other Countries of the Former Soviet Union, edited by Daniel A. Citrin and Ashok K. Lahiri. 1995.

132. Financial Fragilities in Latin America: The 1980s and 1990s, by Liliana Rojas-Suárez and Steven R. Weisbrod. 1995.

131. Capital Account Convertibility: Review of Experience and Implications for IMF Policies, by staff teams headed by Peter J. Quirk and Owen Evans. 1995.

130. Challenges to the Swedish Welfare State, by Desmond Lachman, Adam Bennett, John H. Green, Robert Hagemann, and Ramana Ramaswamy. 1995.

129. IMF Conditionality: Experience Under Stand-By and Extended Arrangements. Part II: Background Papers. Susan Schadler, Editor, with Adam Bennett, Maria Carkovic, Louis Dicks-Mireaux, Mauro Mecagni, James H.J. Morsink, and Miguel A. Savastano. 1995.

128. IMF Conditionality: Experience Under Stand-By and Extended Arrangements. Part I: Key Issues and Findings, by Susan Schadler, Adam Bennett, Maria Carkovic, Louis Dicks-Mireaux, Mauro Mecagni, James H.J. Morsink, and Miguel A. Savastano. 1995.

127. Road Maps of the Transition: The Baltics, the Czech Republic, Hungary, and Russia, by Biswajit Banerjee, Vincent Koen, Thomas Krueger, Mark S. Lutz, Michael Marrese, and Tapio O. Saavalainen. 1995.

126. The Adoption of Indirect Instruments of Monetary Policy, by a Staff Team headed by William E. Alexander, Tomás J.T. Baliño, and Charles Enoch. 1995.

125. United Germany: The First Five Years—Performance and Policy Issues, by Robert Corker, Robert A. Feldman, Karl Habermeier, Hari Vittas, and Tessa van der Willigen. 1995.

124. Saving Behavior and the Asset Price "Bubble" in Japan: Analytical Studies, edited by Ulrich Baumgartner and Guy Meredith. 1995.

123. Comprehensive Tax Reform: The Colombian Experience, edited by Parthasarathi Shome. 1995.

122. Capital Flows in the APEC Region, edited by Mohsin S. Khan and Carmen M. Reinhart. 1995.

121. Uganda: Adjustment with Growth, 1987–94, by Robert L. Sharer, Hema R. De Zoysa, and Calvin A. McDonald. 1995.

120. Economic Dislocation and Recovery in Lebanon, by Sena Eken, Paul Cashin, S. Nuri Erbas, Jose Martelino, and Adnan Mazarei. 1995.

119. Singapore: A Case Study in Rapid Development, edited by Kenneth Bercuson with a staff team comprising Robert G. Carling, Aasim M. Husain, Thomas Rumbaugh, and Rachel van Elkan. 1995.

118. Sub-Saharan Africa: Growth, Savings, and Investment, by Michael T. Hadjimichael, Dhaneshwar Ghura, Martin Mühleisen, Roger Nord, and E. Murat Uçer. 1995.

117. Resilience and Growth Through Sustained Adjustment: The Moroccan Experience, by Saleh M. Nsouli, Sena Eken, Klaus Enders, Van-Can Thai, Jörg Decressin, and Filippo Cartiglia, with Janet Bungay. 1995.

116. Improving the International Monetary System: Constraints and Possibilities, by Michael Mussa, Morris Goldstein, Peter B. Clark, Donald J. Mathieson, and Tamim Bayoumi. 1994.

115. Exchange Rates and Economic Fundamentals: A Framework for Analysis, by Peter B. Clark, Leonardo Bartolini, Tamim Bayoumi, and Steven Symansky. 1994.

114. Economic Reform in China: A New Phase, by Wanda Tseng, Hoe Ee Khor, Kalpana Kochhar, Dubravko Mihaljek, and David Burton. 1994.

113. Poland: The Path to a Market Economy, by Liam P. Ebrill, Ajai Chopra, Charalambos Christofides, Paul Mylonas, Inci Otker, and Gerd Schwartz. 1994.

112. The Behavior of Non-Oil Commodity Prices, by Eduardo Borensztein, Mohsin S. Khan, Carmen M. Reinhart, and Peter Wickham. 1994.

111. The Russian Federation in Transition: External Developments, by Benedicte Vibe Christensen. 1994.

110. Limiting Central Bank Credit to the Government: Theory and Practice, by Carlo Cottarelli. 1993.

109. The Path to Convertibility and Growth: The Tunisian Experience, by Saleh M. Nsouli, Sena Eken, Paul Duran, Gerwin Bell, and Zühtü Yücelik. 1993.

108. Recent Experiences with Surges in Capital Inflows, by Susan Schadler, Maria Carkovic, Adam Bennett, and Robert Kahn. 1993.

107. China at the Threshold of a Market Economy, by Michael W. Bell, Hoe Ee Khor, and Kalpana Kochhar with Jun Ma, Simon N'guiamba, and Rajiv Lall. 1993.

106. Economic Adjustment in Low-Income Countries: Experience Under the Enhanced Structural Adjustment Facility, by Susan Schadler, Franek Rozwadowski, Siddharth Tiwari, and David O. Robinson. 1993.

105. The Structure and Operation of the World Gold Market, by Gary O'Callaghan. 1993.

104. Price Liberalization in Russia: Behavior of Prices, Household Incomes, and Consumption During the First Year, by Vincent Koen and Steven Phillips. 1993.

103. Liberalization of the Capital Account: Experiences and Issues, by Donald J. Mathieson and Liliana Rojas-Suárez. 1993.

102. Financial Sector Reforms and Exchange Arrangements in Eastern Europe. Part I: Financial Markets and Intermediation, by Guillermo A. Calvo and Manmohan S. Kumar. Part II: Exchange Arrangements of Previously Centrally Planned Economies, by Eduardo Borensztein and Paul R. Masson. 1993.

101. Spain: Converging with the European Community, by Michel Galy, Gonzalo Pastor, and Thierry Pujol. 1993.

100. The Gambia: Economic Adjustment in a Small Open Economy, by Michael T. Hadjimichael, Thomas Rumbaugh, and Eric Verreydt. 1992.

99. Mexico: The Strategy to Achieve Sustained Economic Growth, edited by Claudio Loser and Eliot Kalter. 1992.

98. Albania: From Isolation Toward Reform, by Mario I. Blejer, Mauro Mecagni, Ratna Sahay, Richard Hides, Barry Johnston, Piroska Nagy, and Roy Pepper. 1992.

97. Rules and Discretion in International Economic Policy, by Manuel Guitián. 1992.

Note: For information on the title and availability of Occasional Papers not listed, please consult the IMF Publications Catalog or contact IMF Publication Services.